Coloring Book

Mindfulness

for Adults

Welcome to the world of beauty, harmony, relaxation, and transformation. This book features 50 unique mandala pattern designs that will enchant you with their imagery and harmony. Immerse yourself in the world of beauty, harmony, and transformation. BEAUTY TRANSFORMS THE SOUL! The black background of the pages is gentle on the eyes, aiding in relaxation. A colored mandala on a black background makes it more unique and vibrant. The interplay of colors in its beauty makes it magically appealing. The mandala's lines are designed to allow any colors, even seemingly mismatched ones. Everything in the mandala will be harmonious and beautiful. After working with the book, you can frame each page and admire your creativity for a long time. Each mandala image has its unique features! A mandala with an empty center can absorb negative energy, regardless of its color scheme. A mandala with a clear center can fill the space, it occupies, with energy. You can create a mandala in a color scheme that resonates with the energy you wish to receive. You can use color schemes corresponding to chakras or planets, adjusting and harmonizing your subtle bodies and space.

Cover by Shelby Hawks
Illustrations by Shelby Hawks

This book belongs to:

Here are some useful tips and hints for working with this book:

1. Use a backing sheet: When working with markers, especially alcohol-based ones, it is recommended to use a backing sheet under the page. This will help prevent the paint from seeping onto the following pages.

2. Choose the right tools: Various tools, such as colored pencils, gel pens, markers, and highlighters, are available for your creativity. However, when using markers, make sure they do not bleed through the paper, for which it is better to use a backing sheet.

3. Experiment with color schemes: Explore different color schemes that correspond to chakras or choose colors that appeal to you. This can add additional value to your coloring process and enhance the energy of your creativity.

4. Take care of your eyes: Since you are working with a black background, this can reduce eye strain and make your coloring more enjoyable and comfortable.

5. Give as a gift or share: Additionally, remember that this book can be used as a wonderful gift for friends and family. Share your creations with others or make video reviews to share your experience with fellow mandala coloring enthusiasts.

I hope these tips will help you fully enjoy the creative process with this book!

With love and best wishes for success,

your Shelby Hawks!

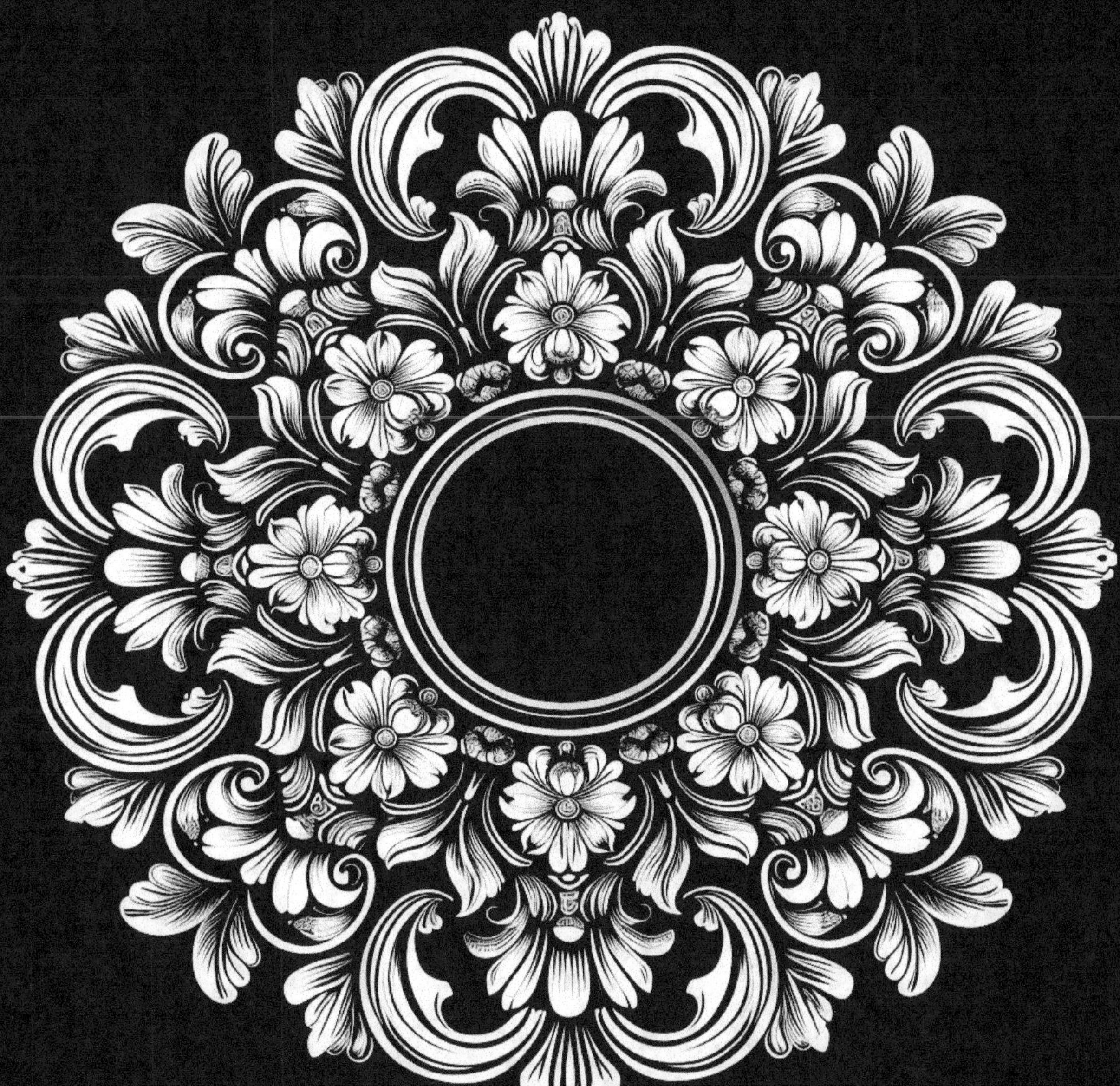

Beauty
transforms
the Soul

Beauty transforms the Soul

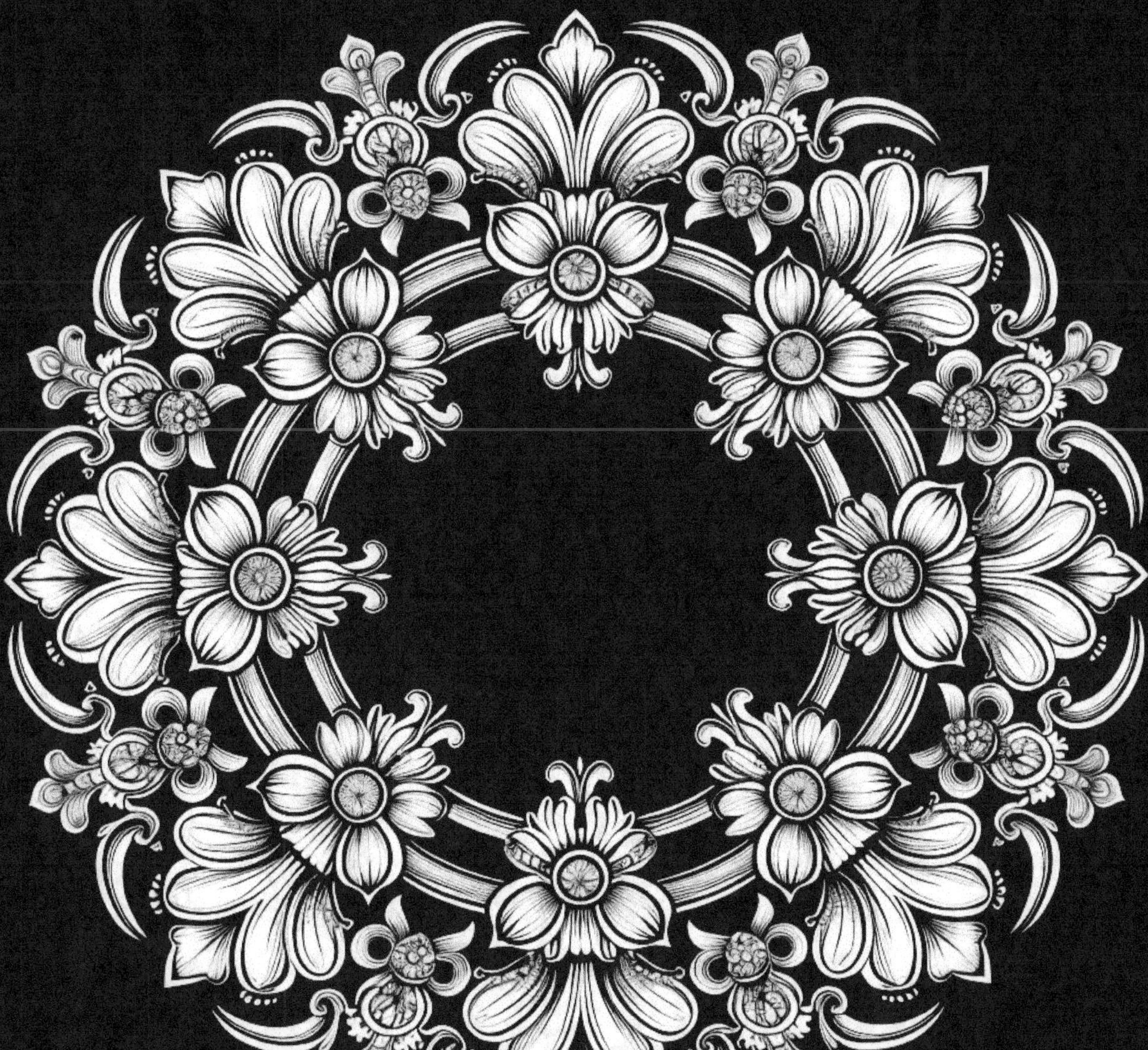

Beauty
transforms
the Soul

Beauty transforms the Soul

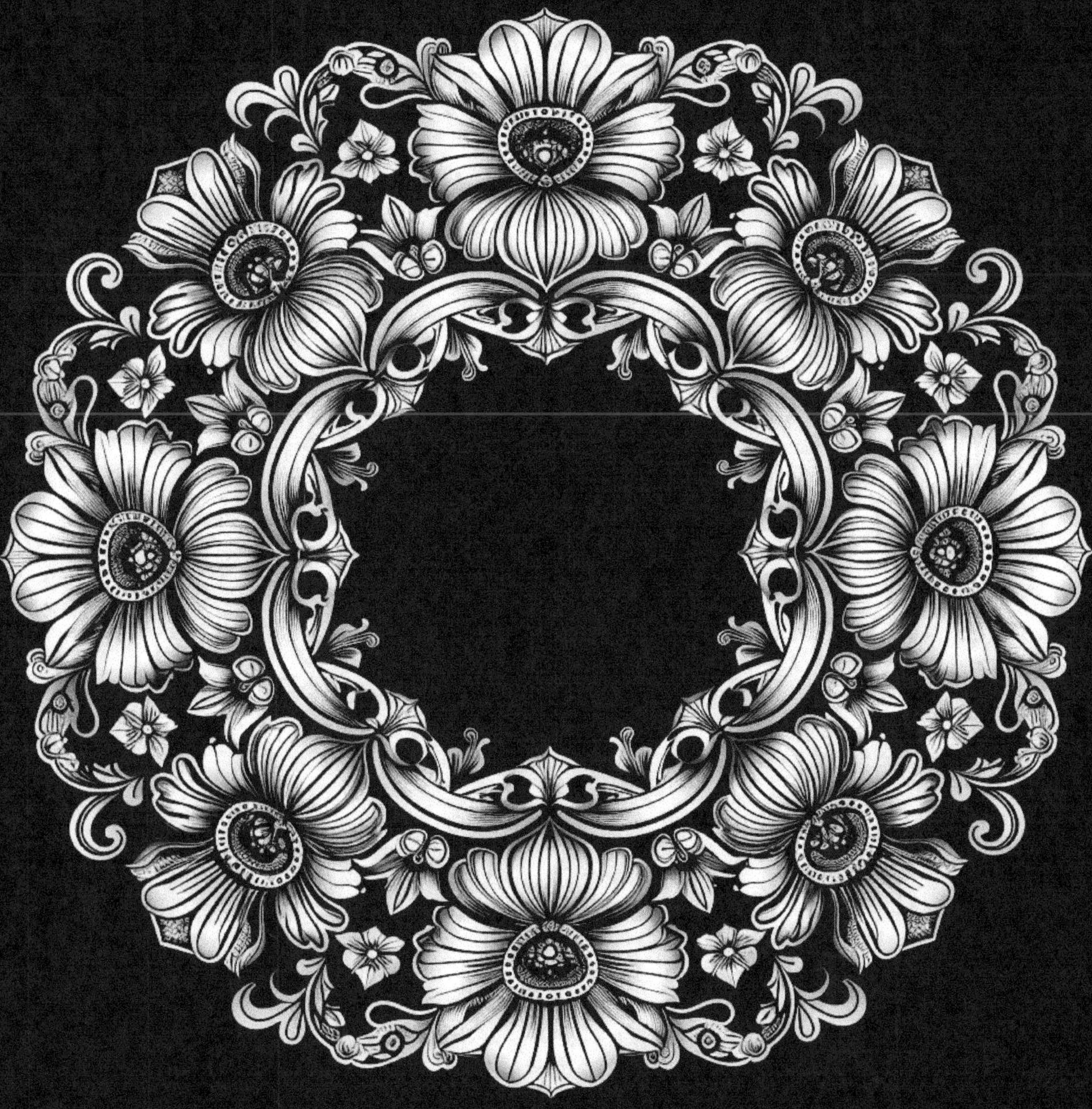

Beauty
transforms
the Soul

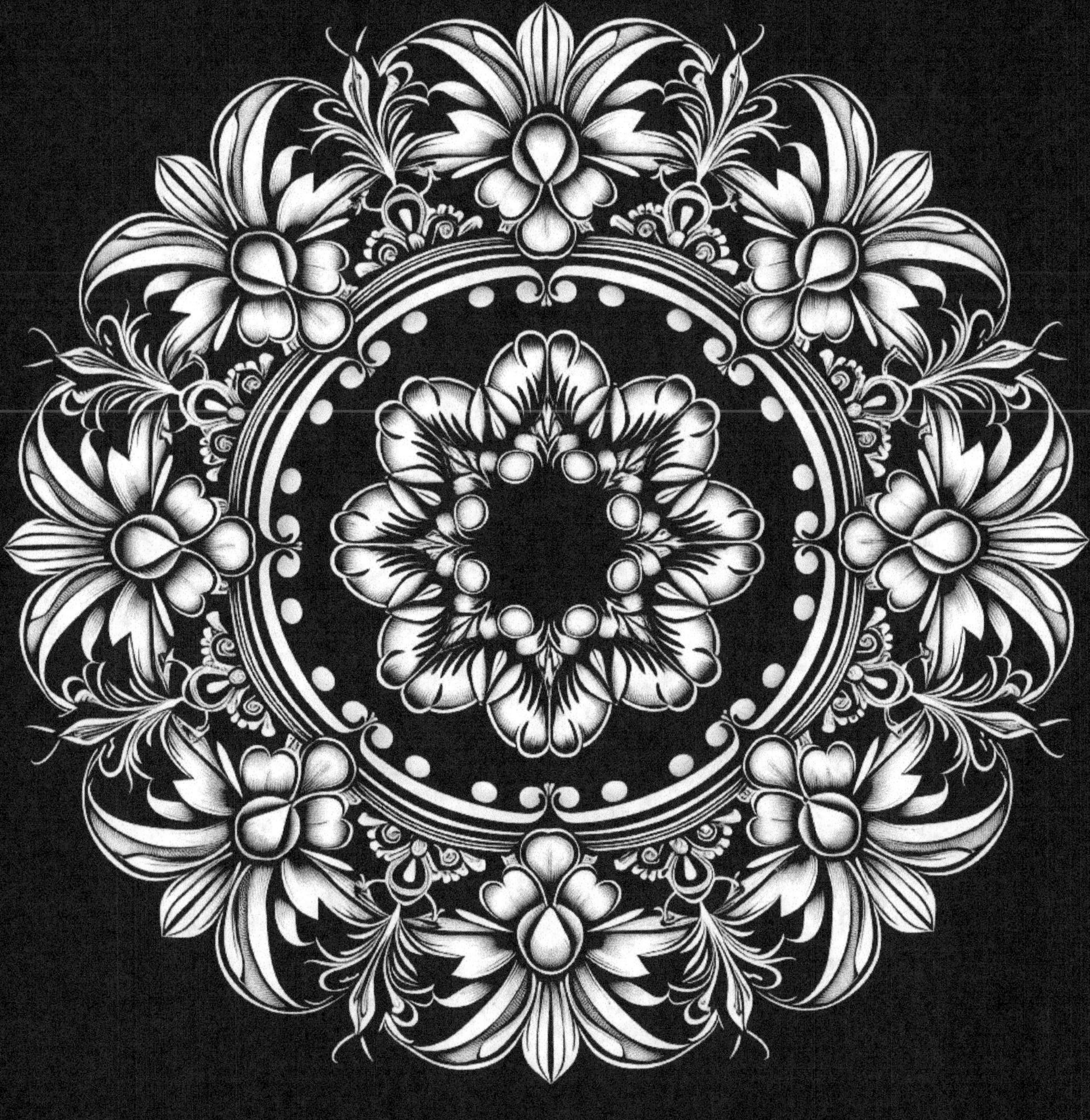

Beauty
transforms
the Soul

Beauty transforms the Soul

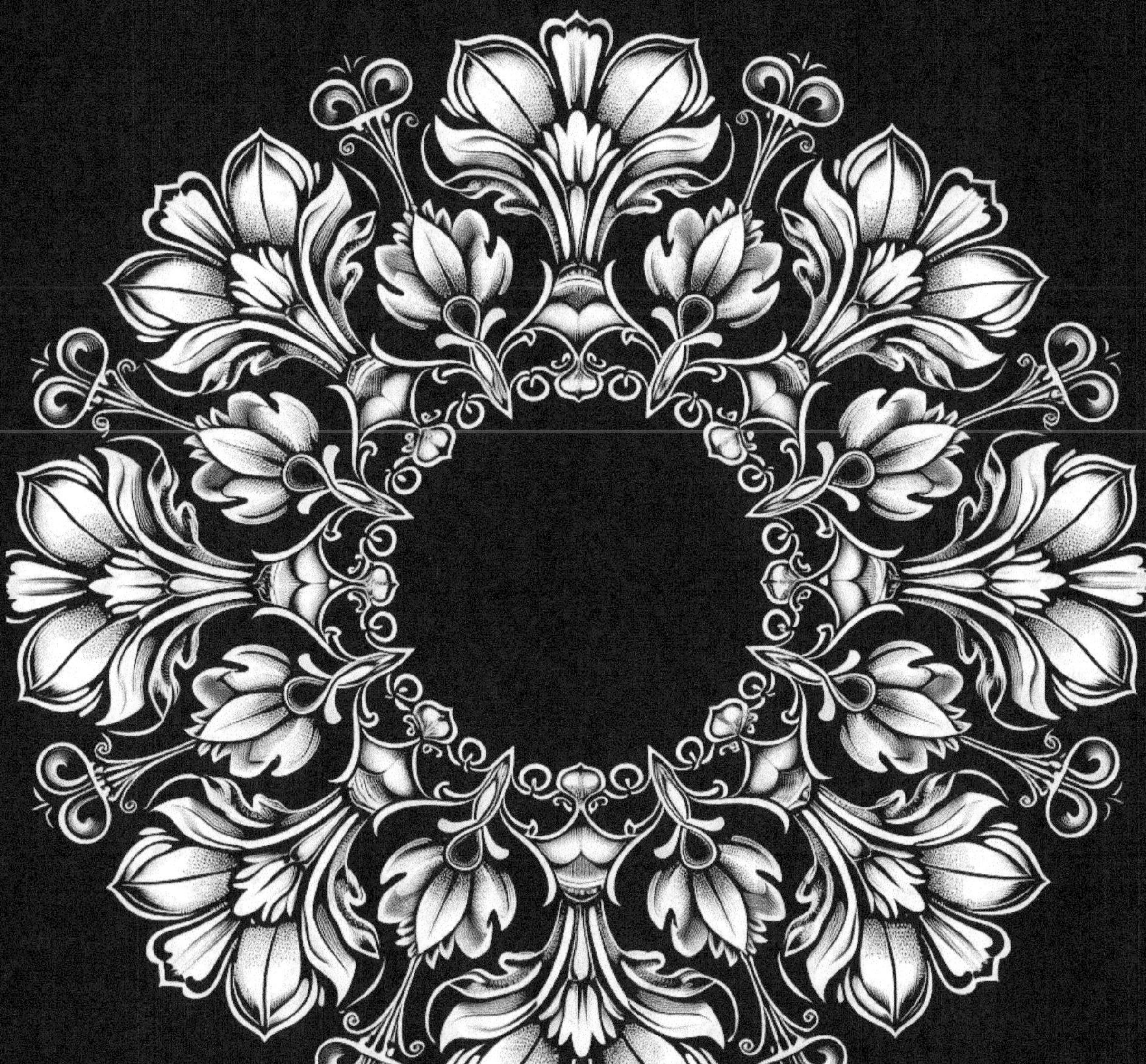

Beauty
transforms
the Soul

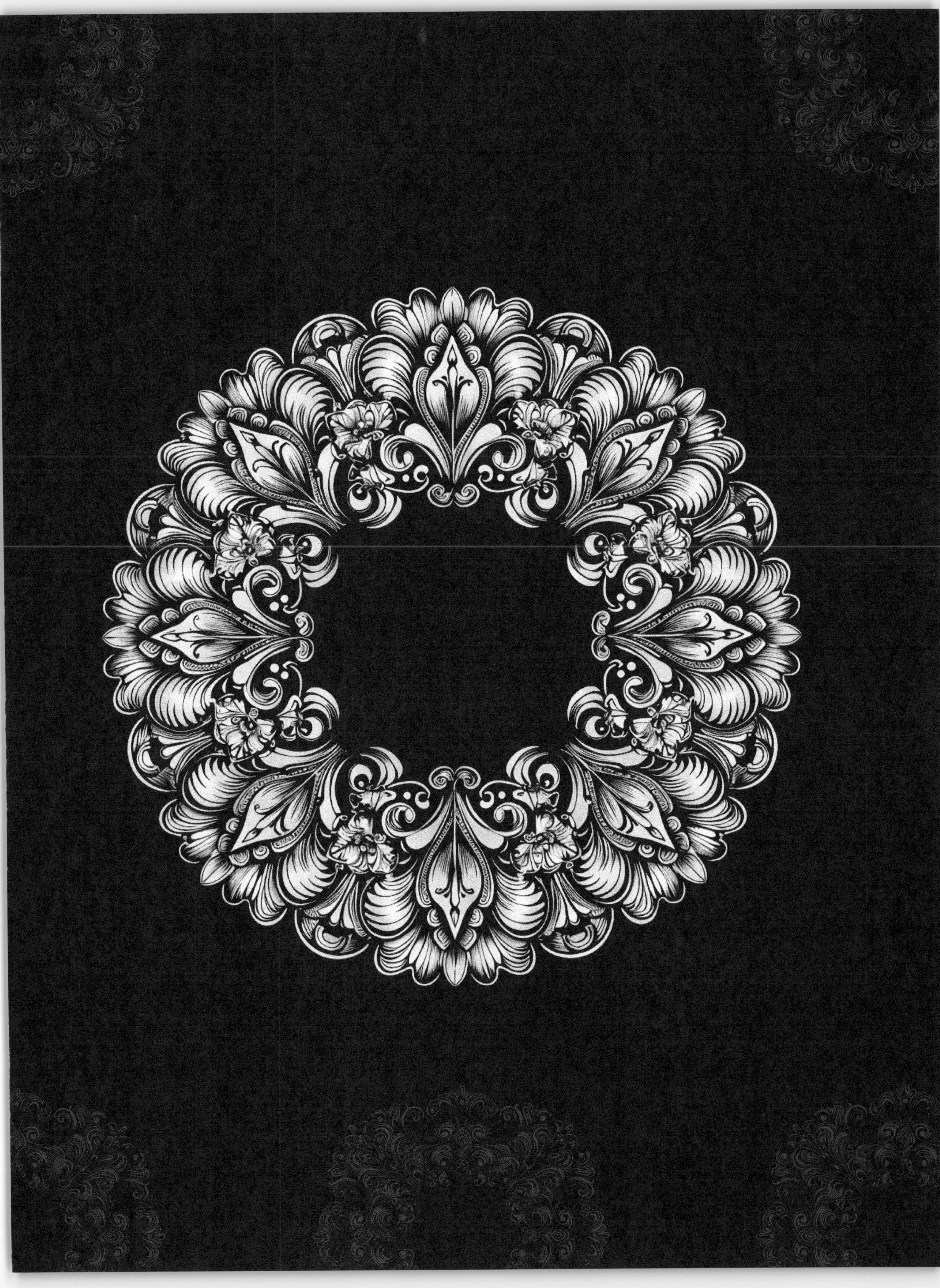

Beauty

transforms

the Soul

Beauty
transforms
the Soul

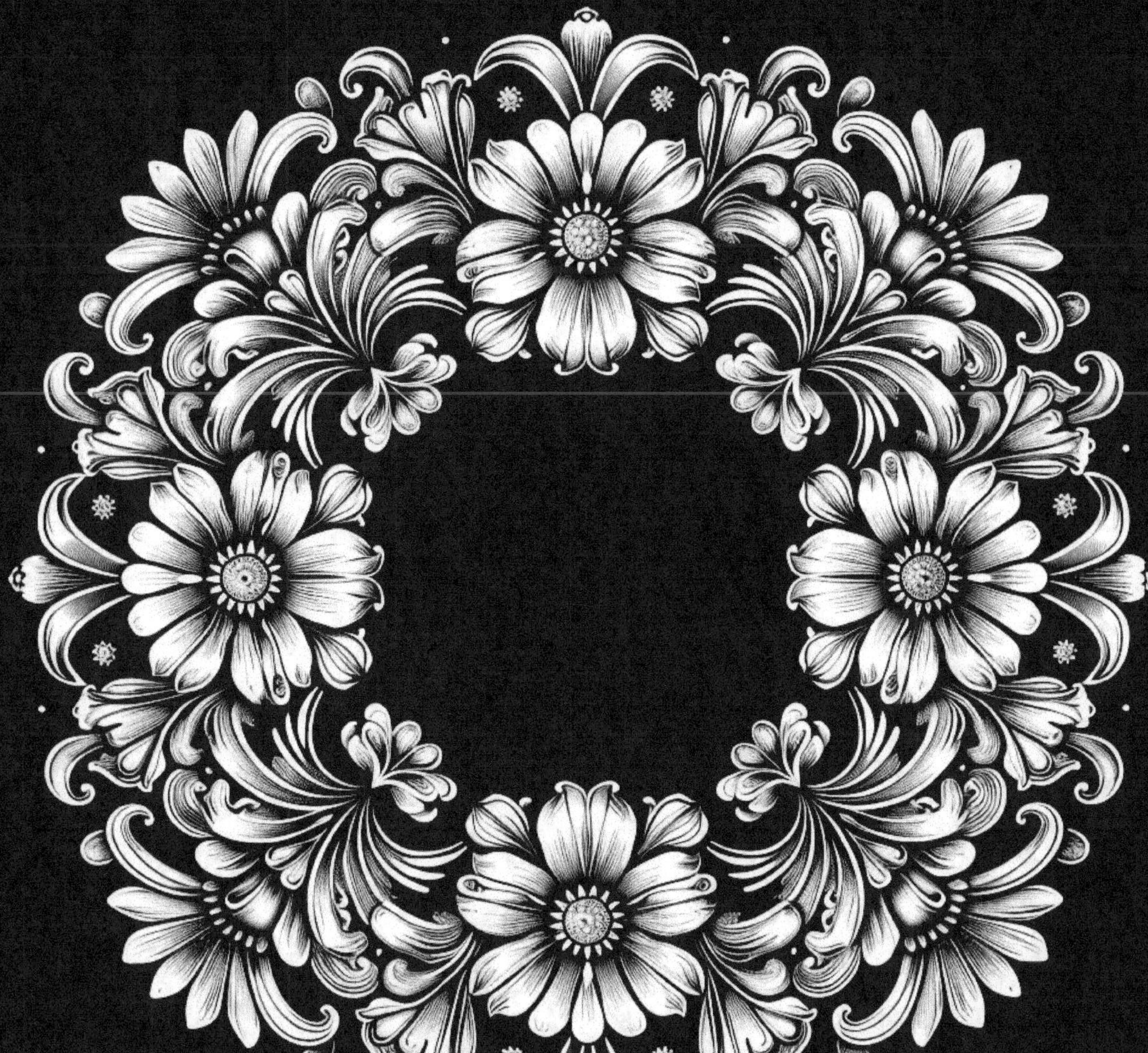

Beauty
transforms
the Soul

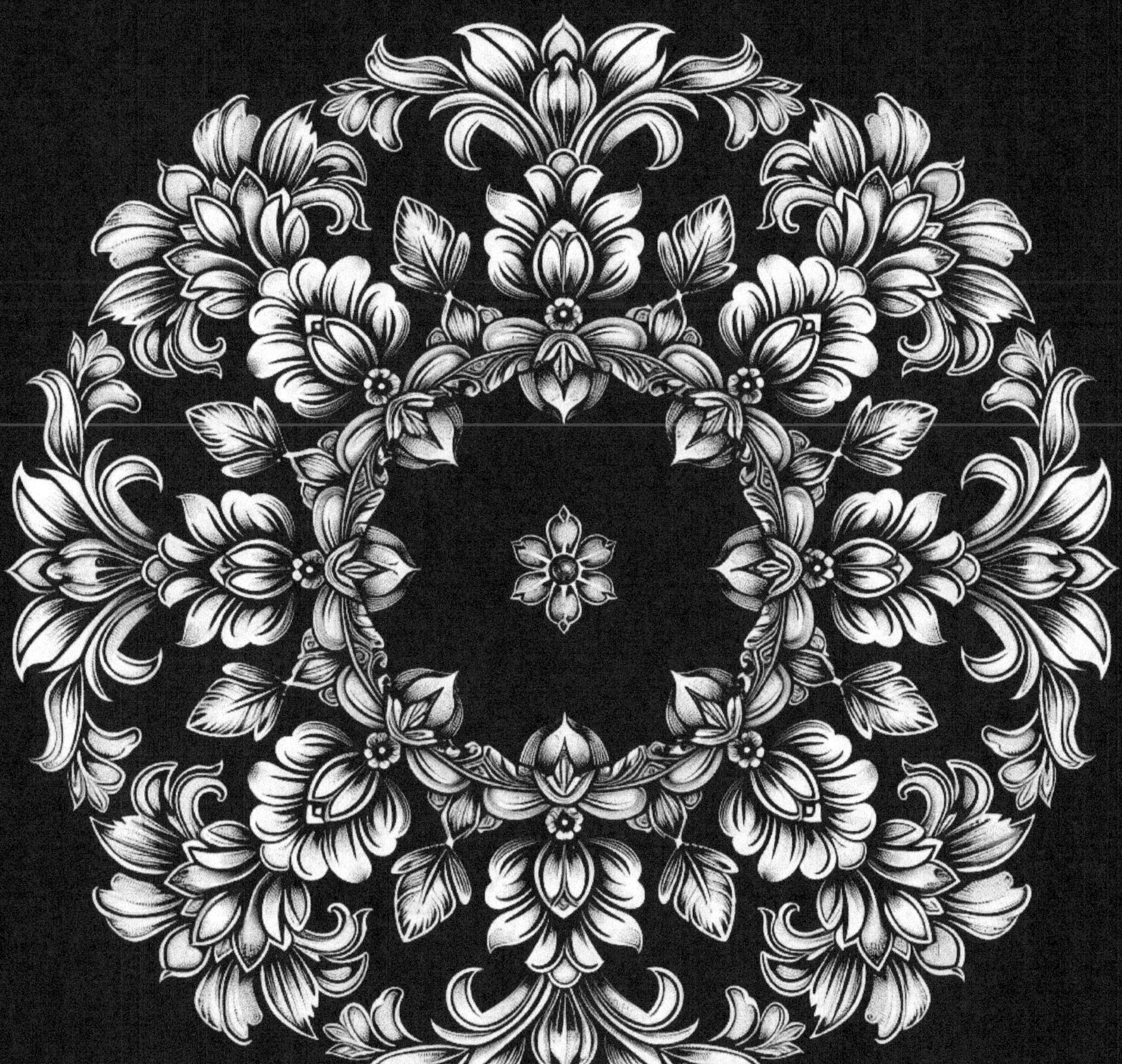

Beauty transforms the Soul

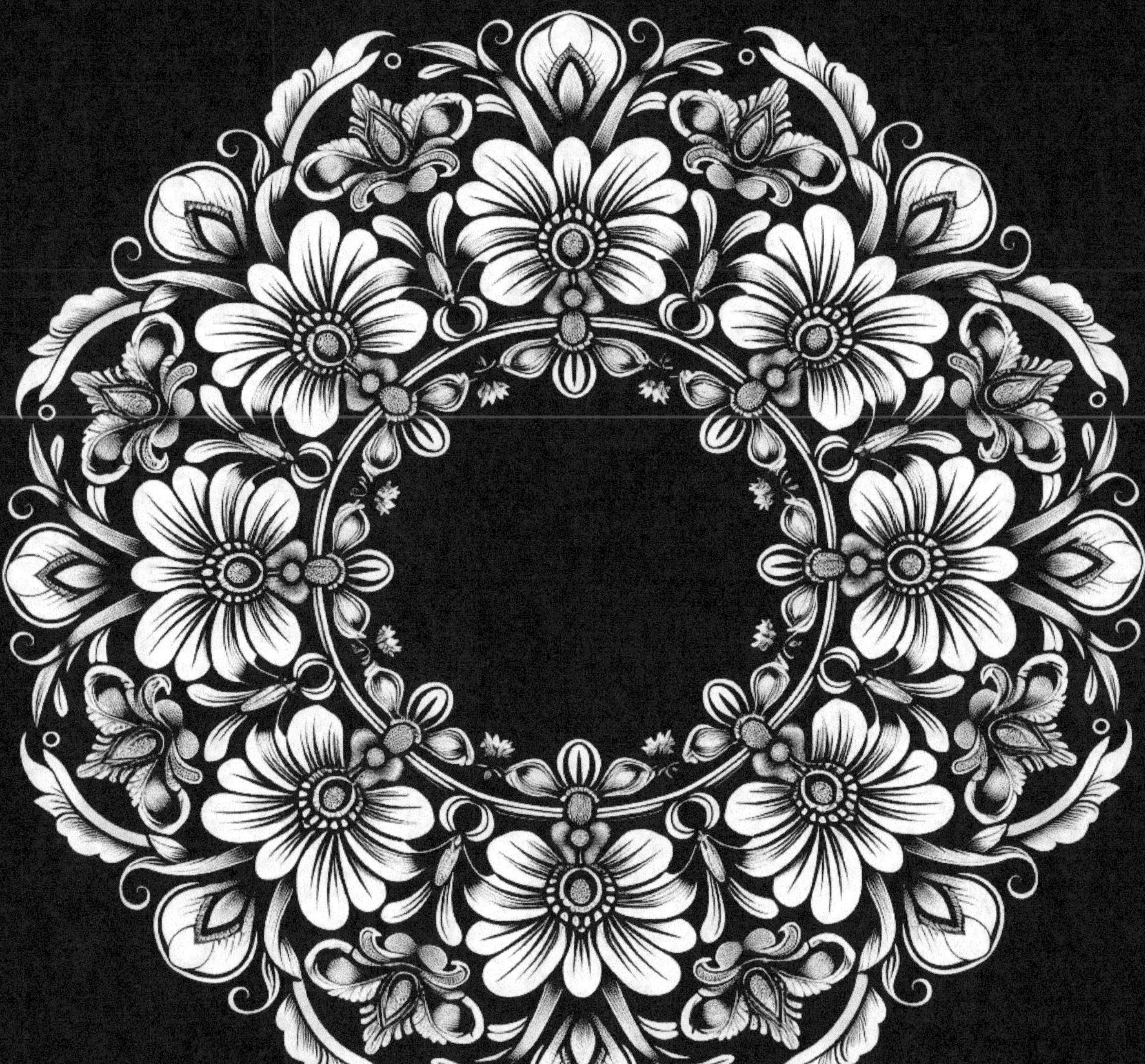

Beauty
transforms
the Soul

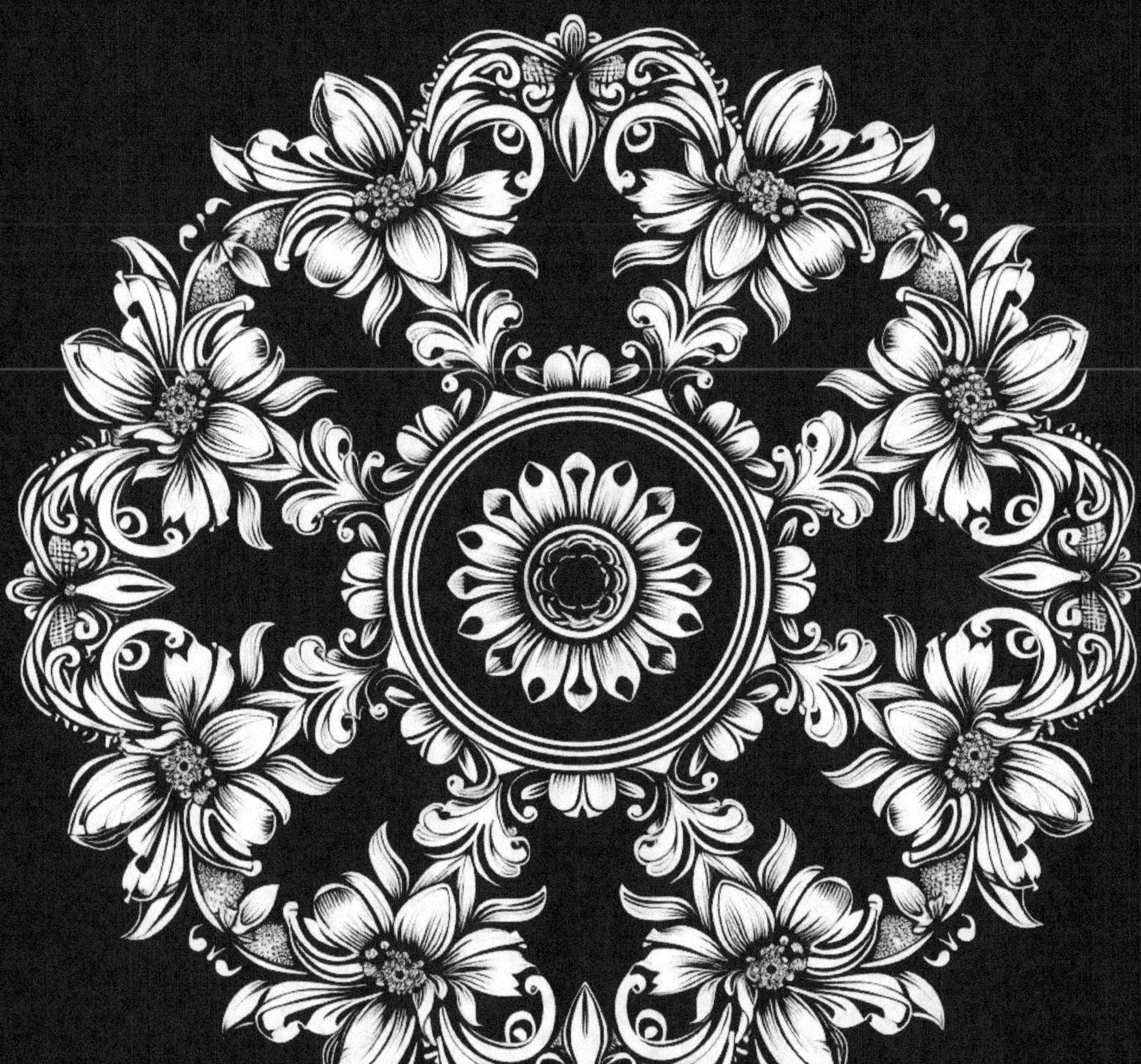

Beauty
transforms
the Soul

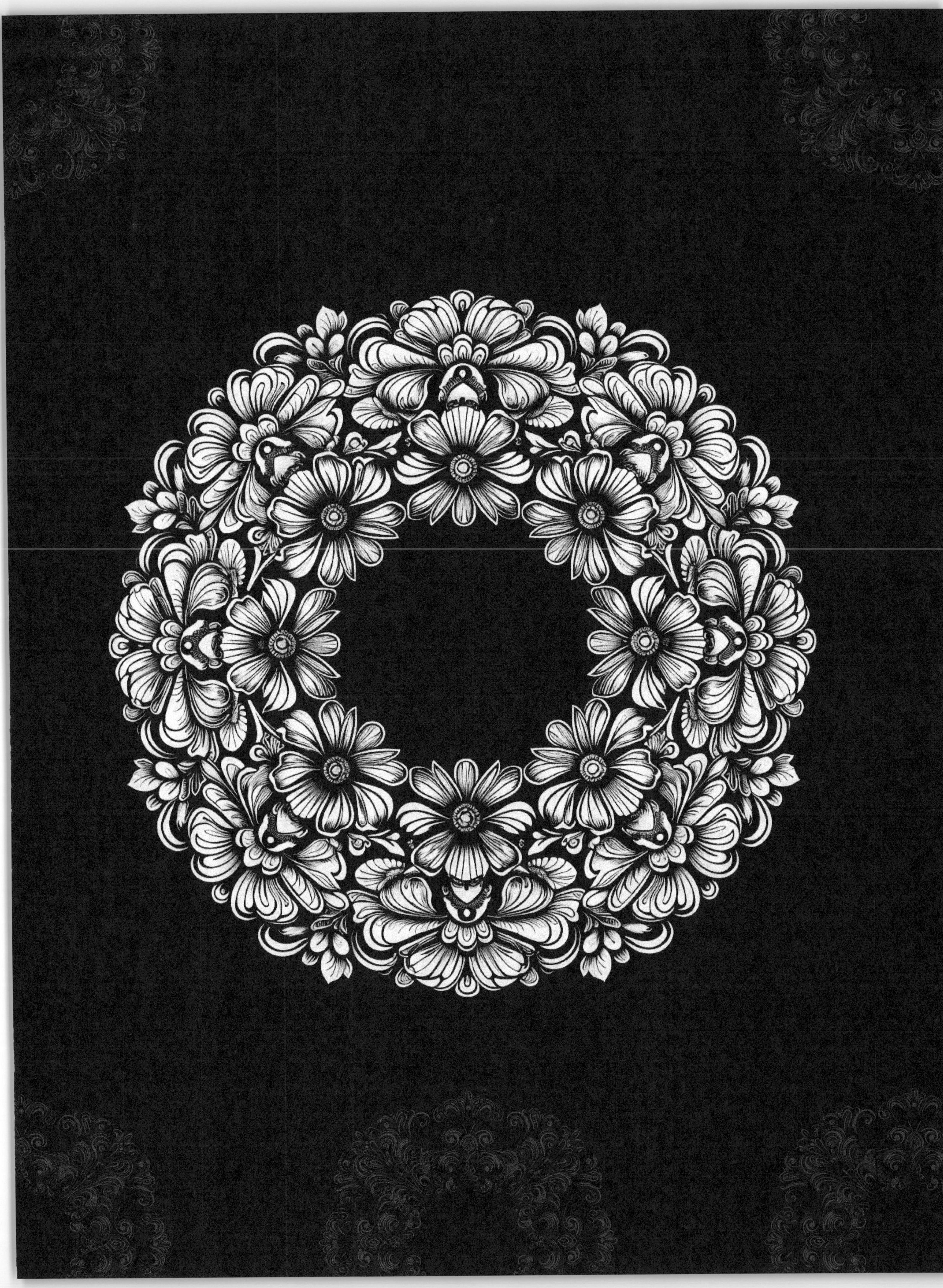

Beauty
transforms
the Soul

Beauty
transforms
the Soul

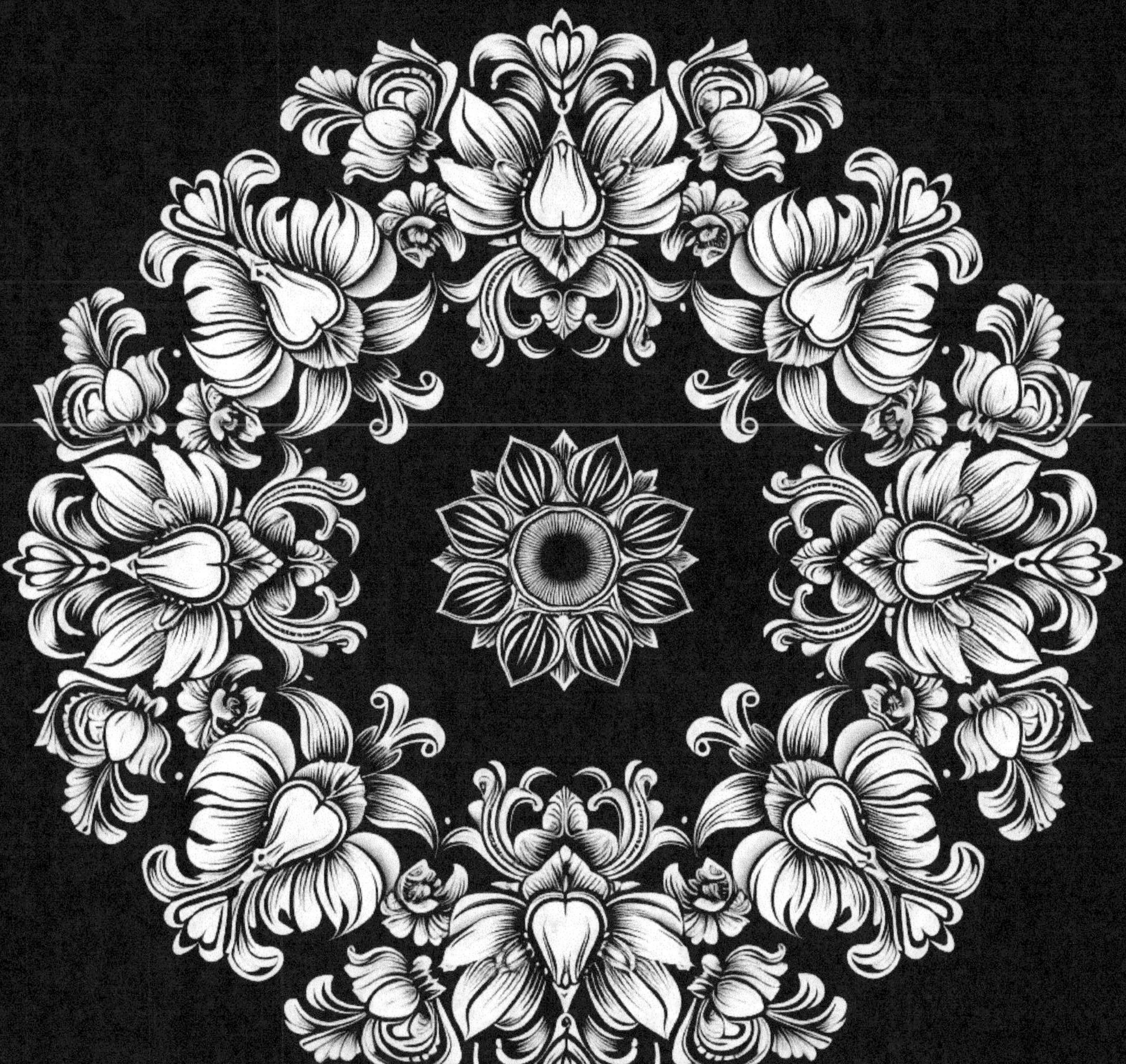

Beauty transforms the Soul

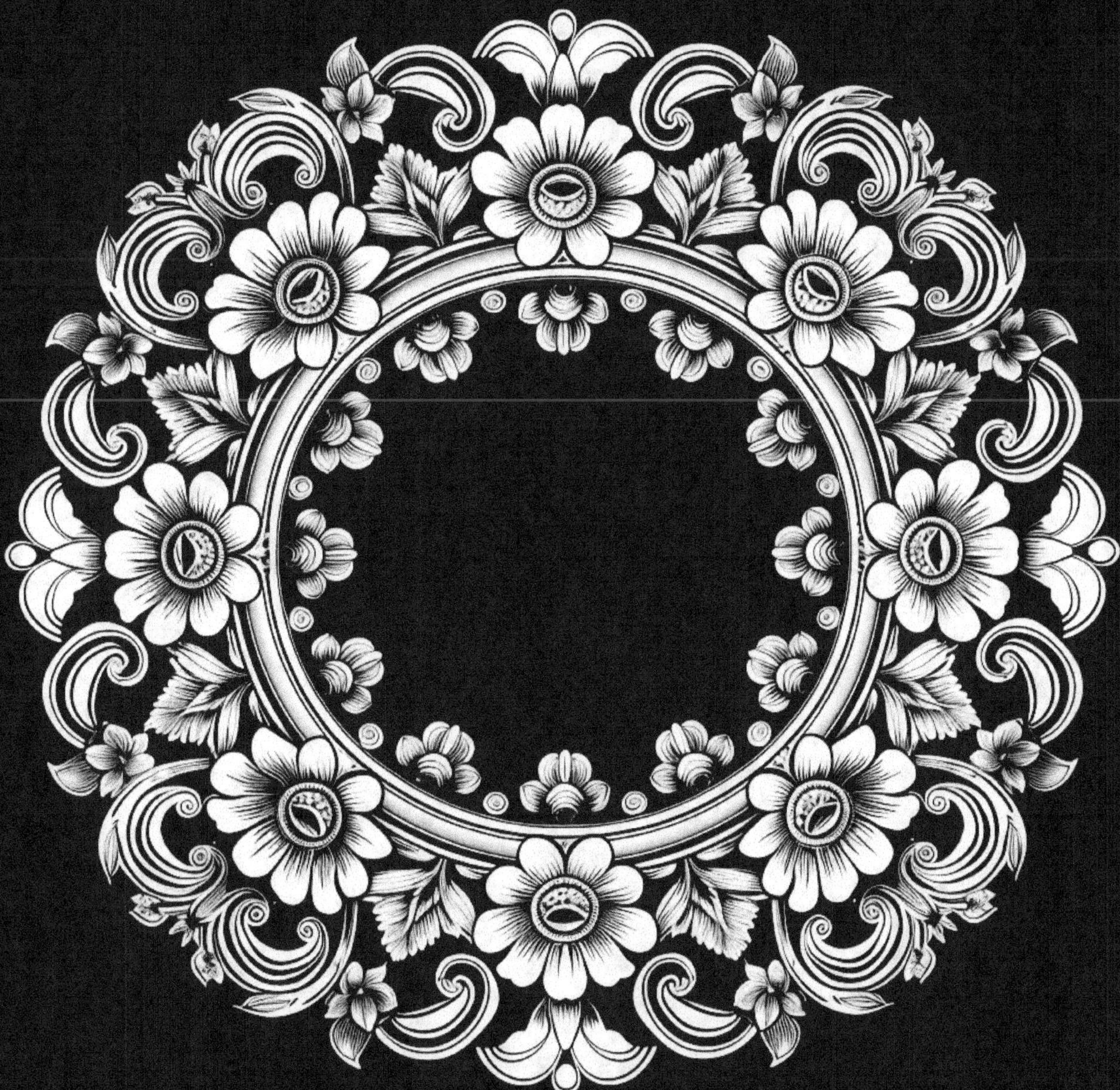

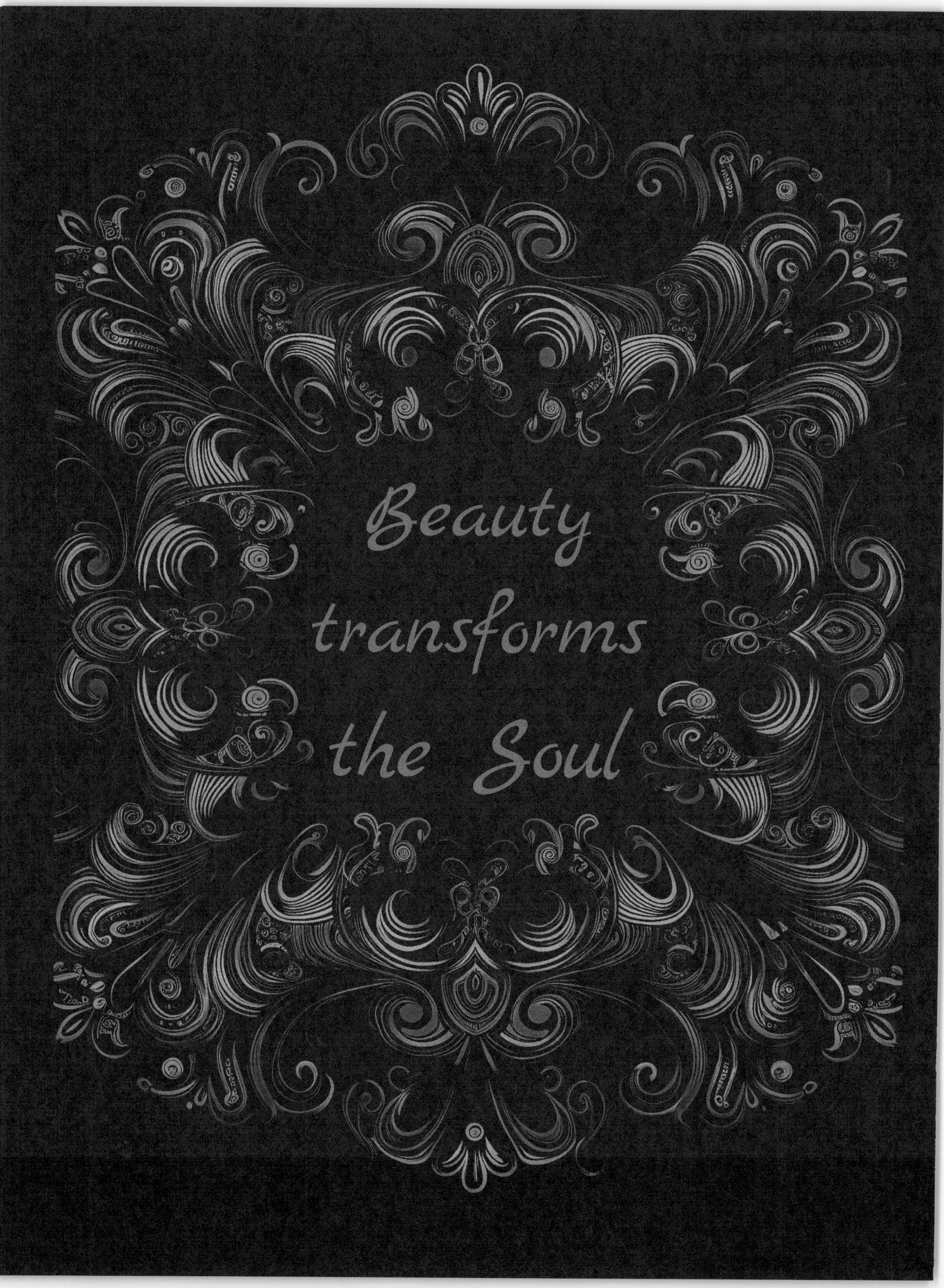
Beauty
transforms
the Soul

Beauty
transforms
the Soul

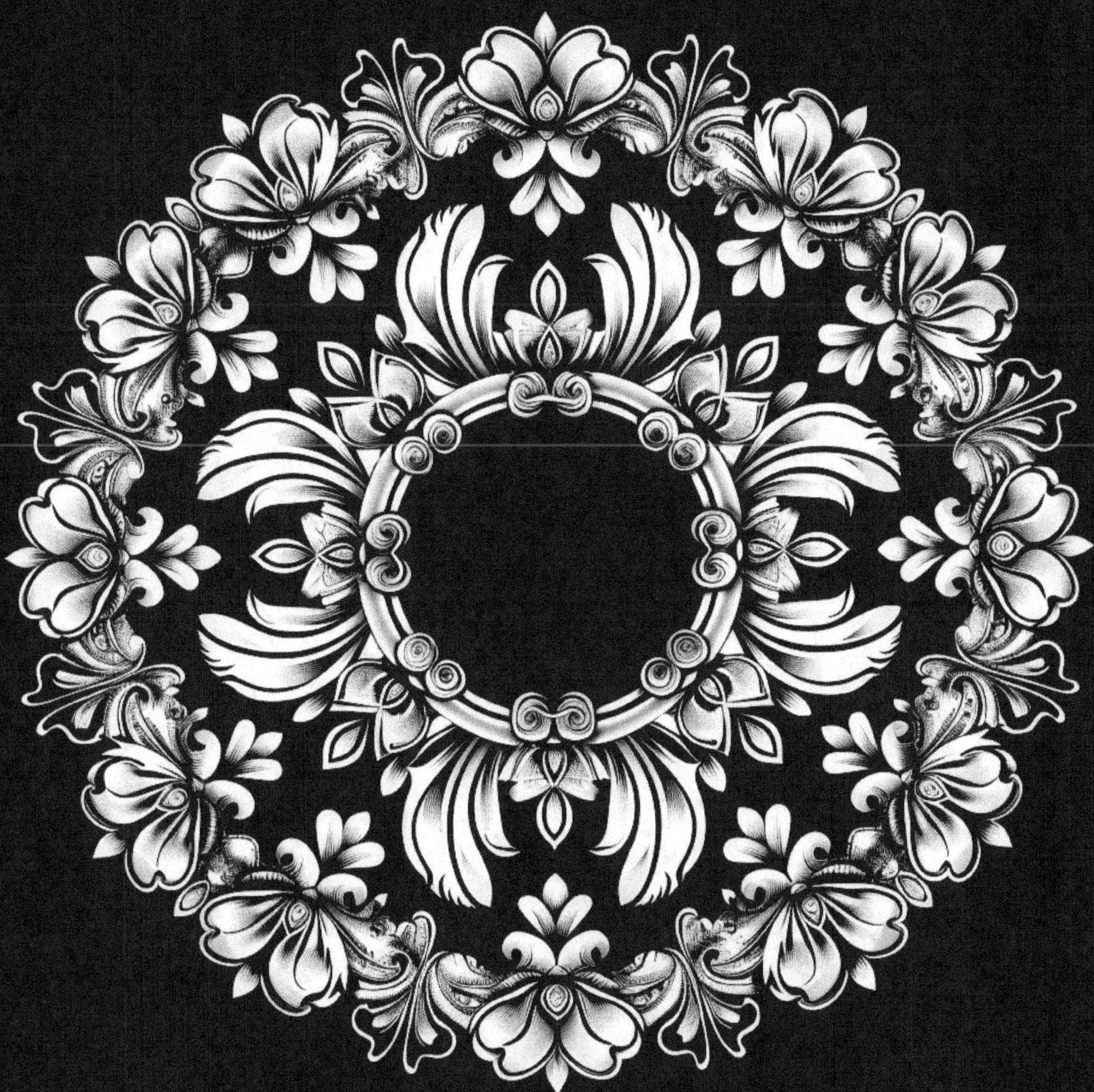

Beauty transforms the Soul

Beauty
transforms
the Soul

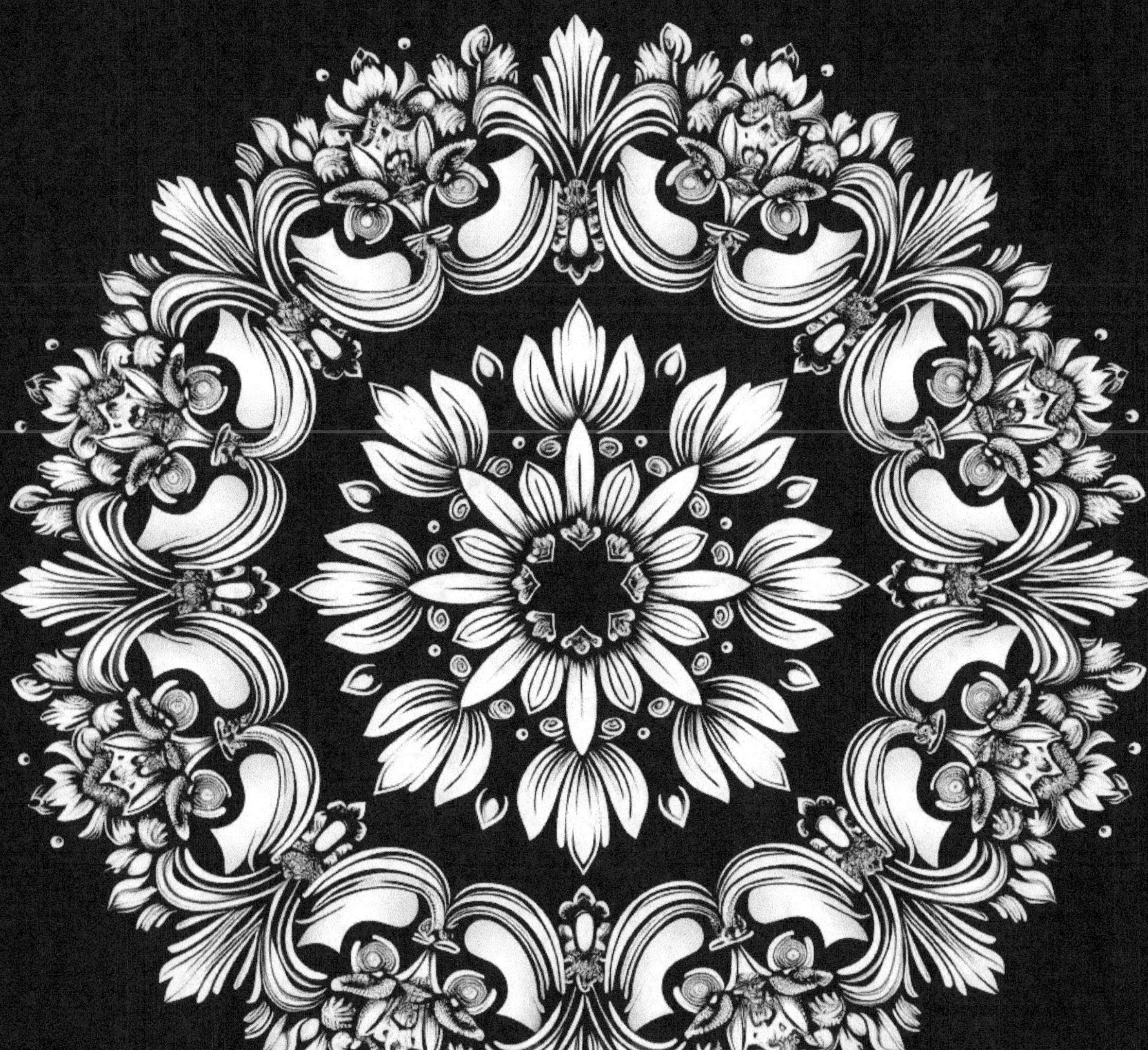

Beauty
transforms
the Soul

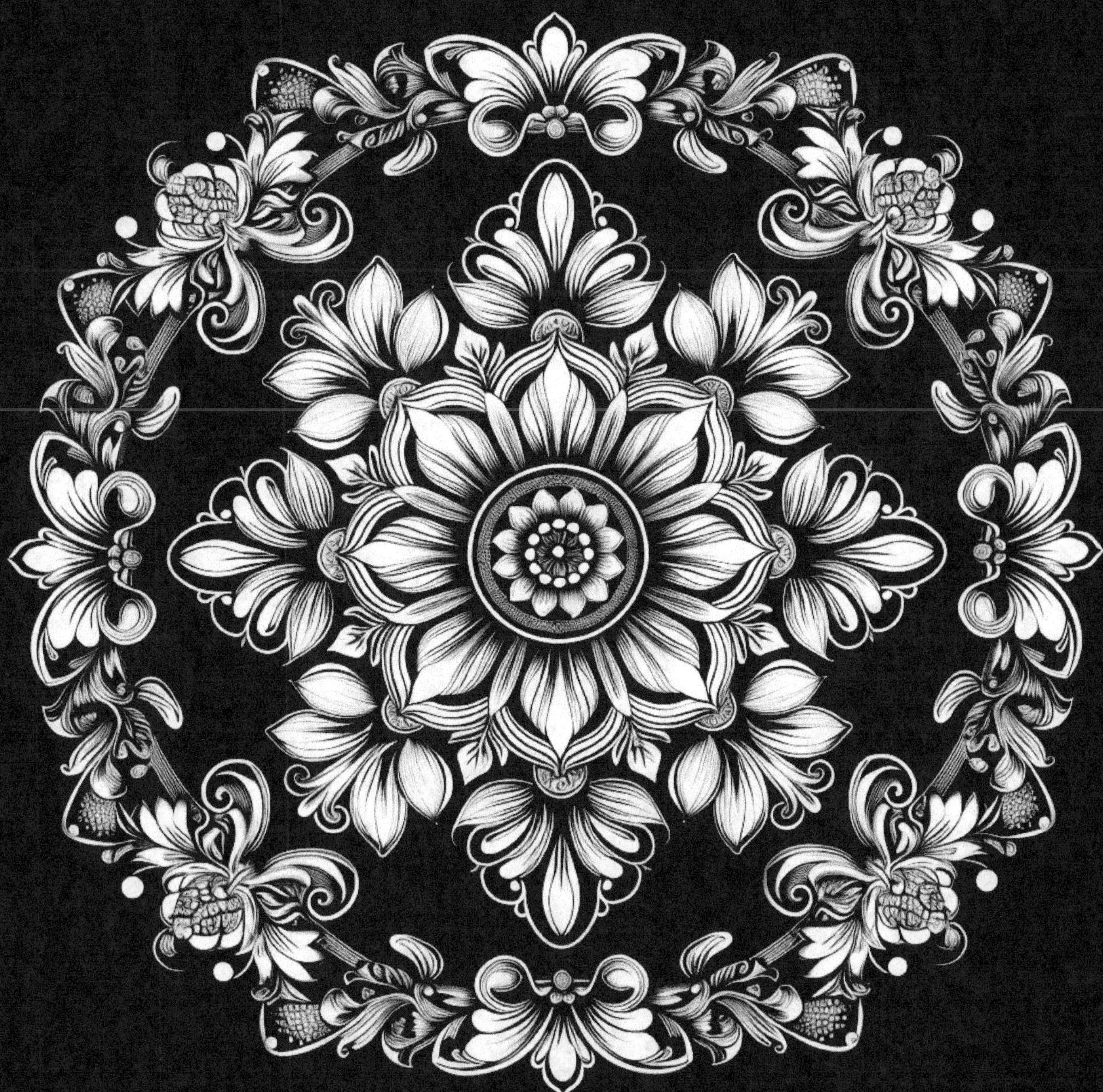

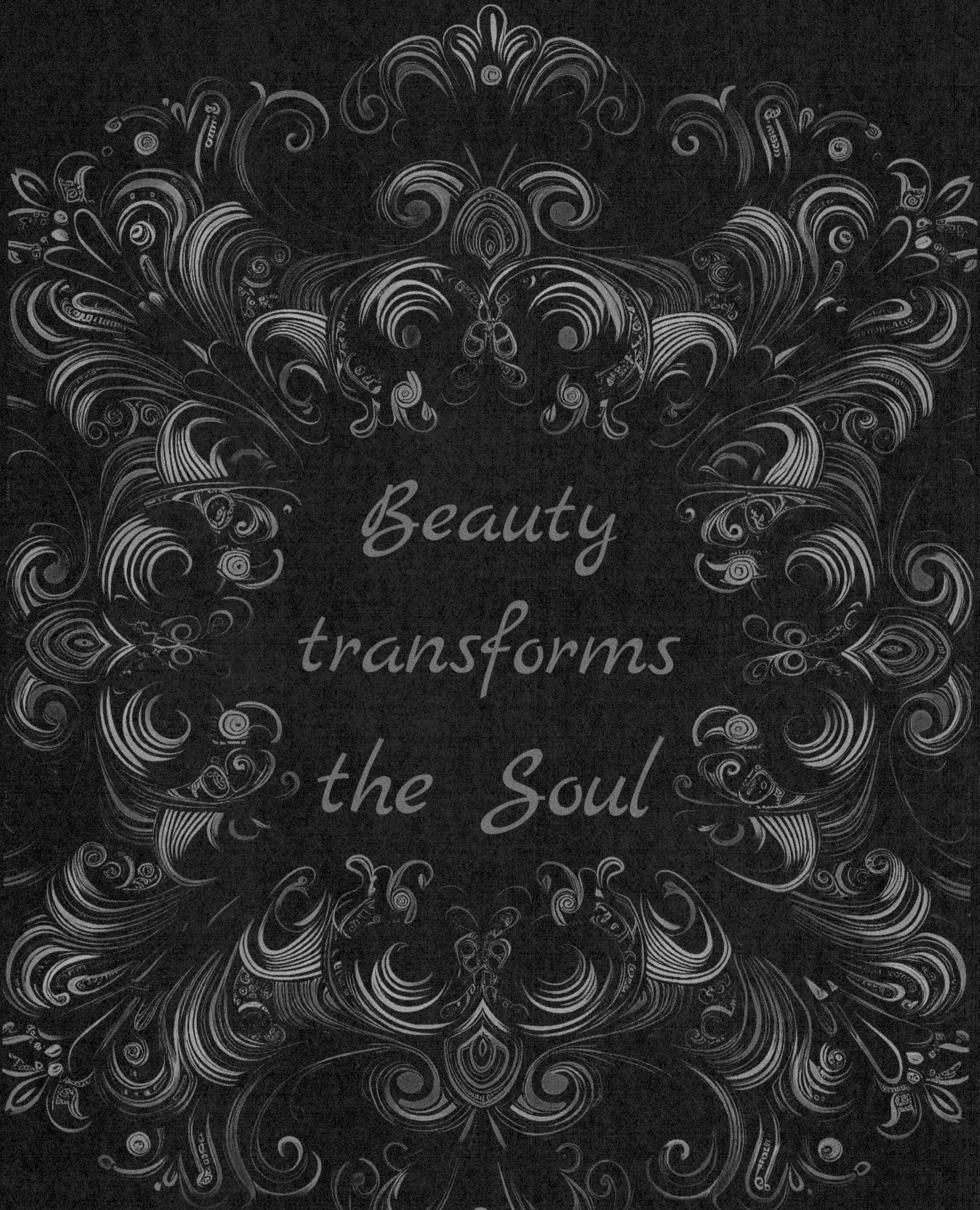
Beauty
transforms
the Soul

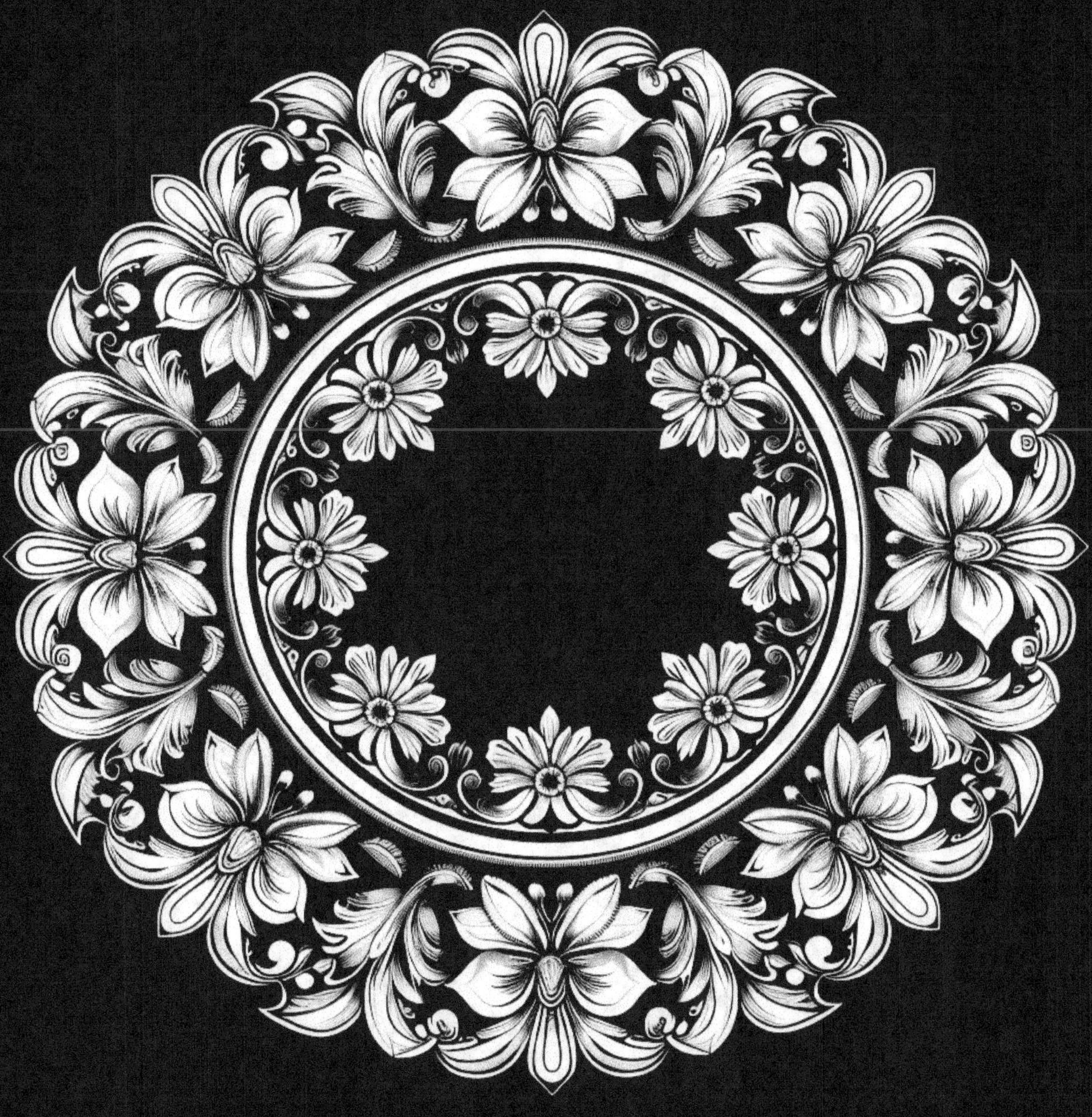

Beauty
transforms
the Soul

Beauty
transforms
the Soul

Beauty
transforms
the Soul

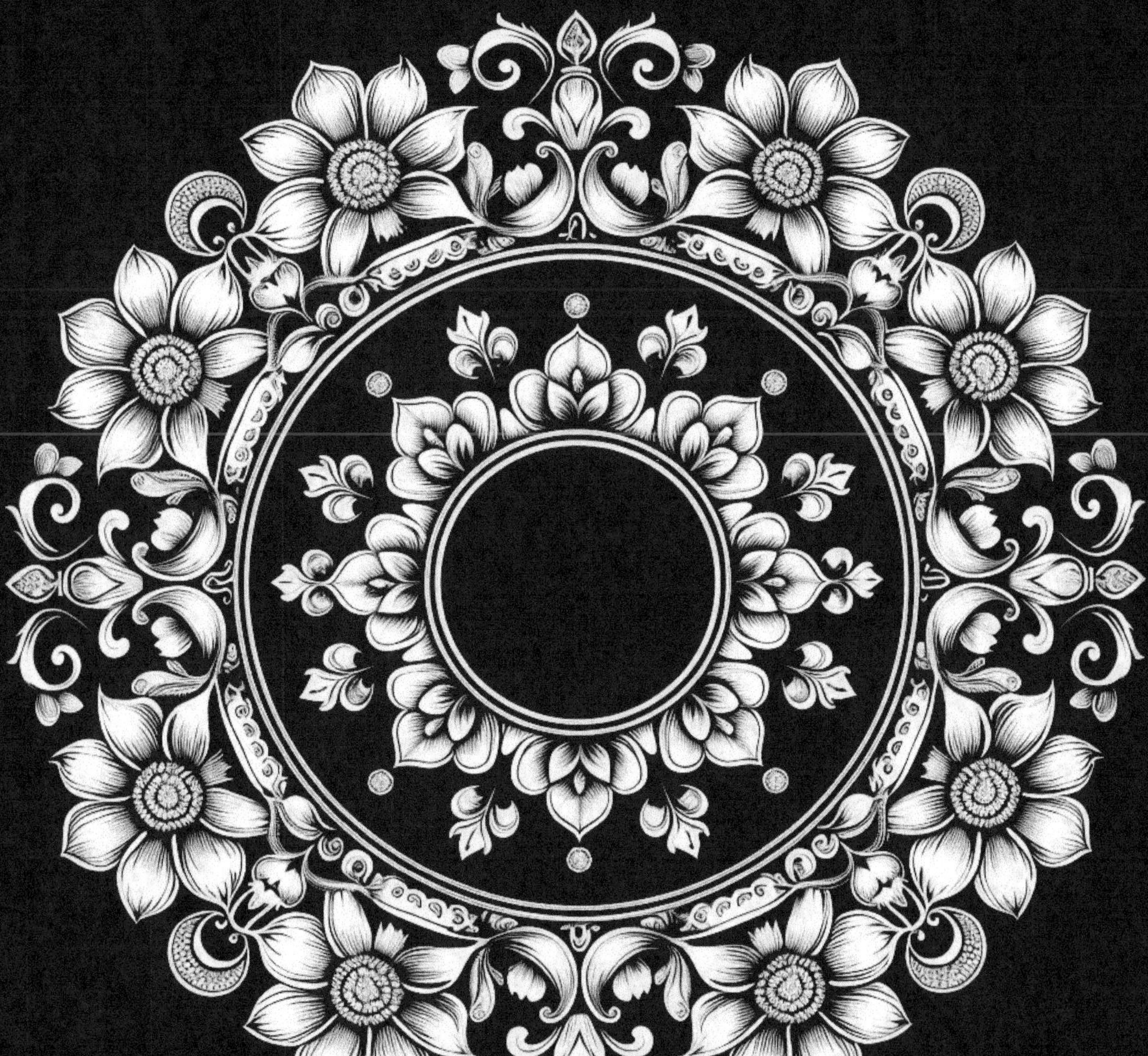

Beauty
transforms
the Soul

Beauty
transforms
the Soul

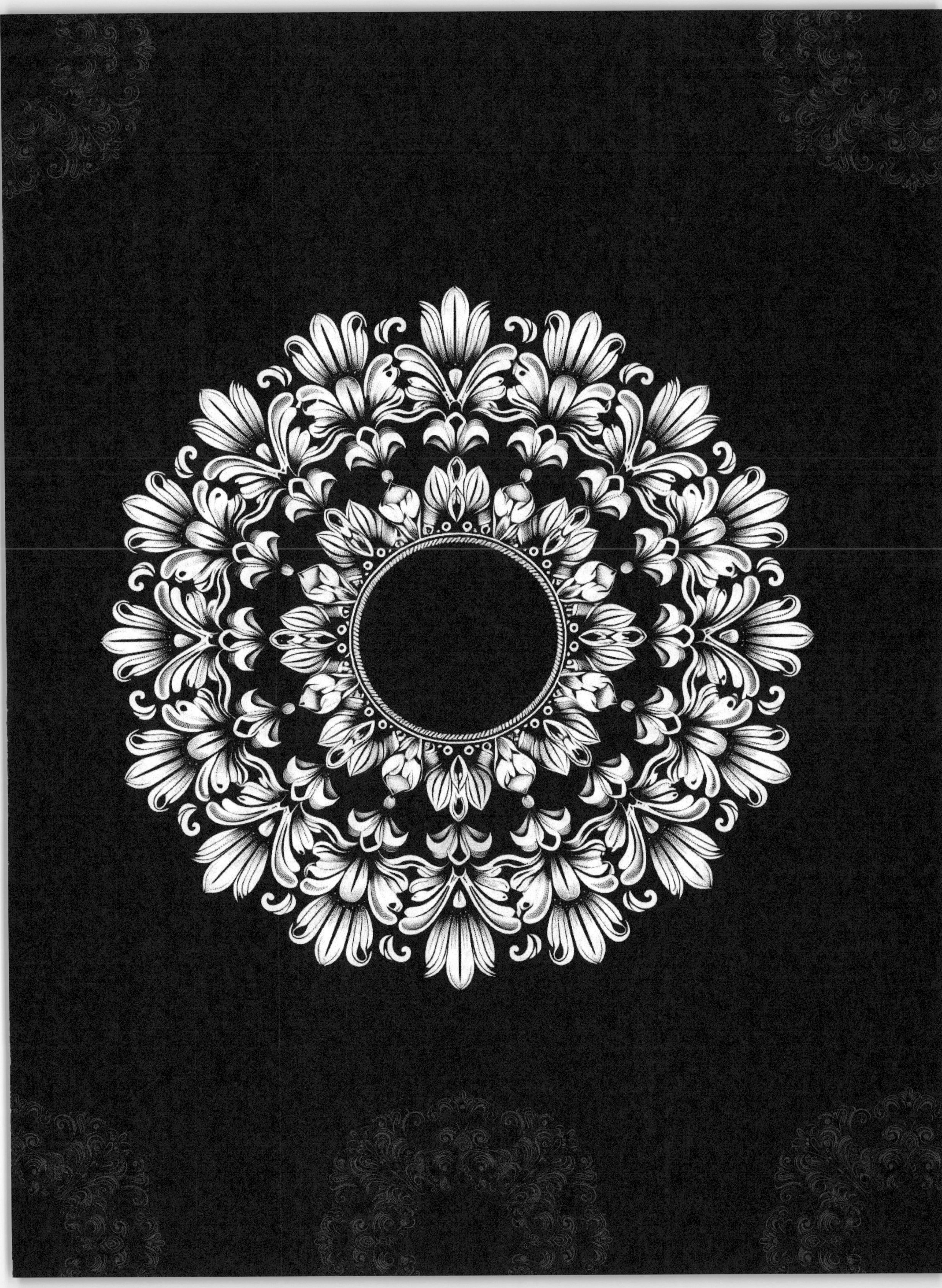

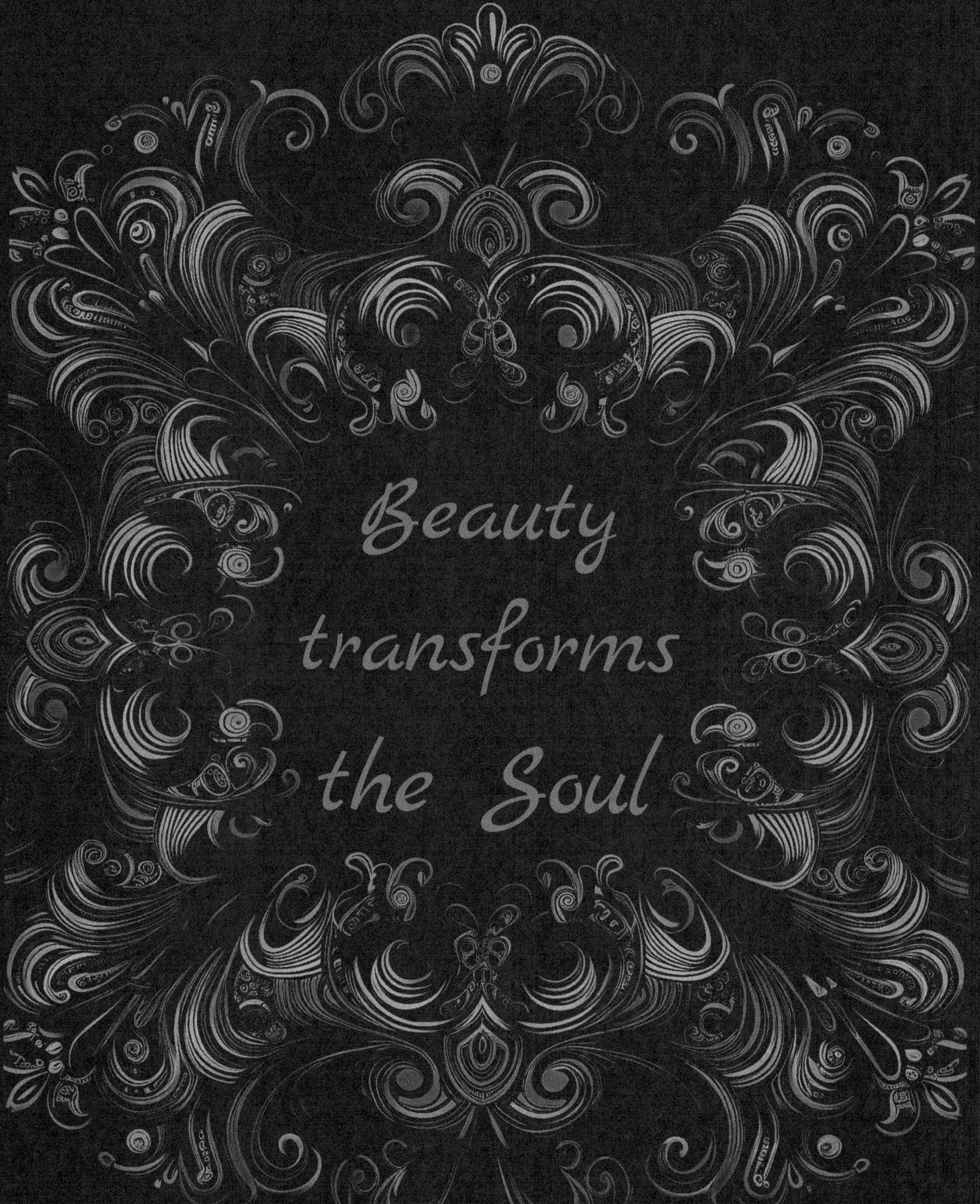
Beauty
transforms
the Soul

Beauty
transforms
the Soul

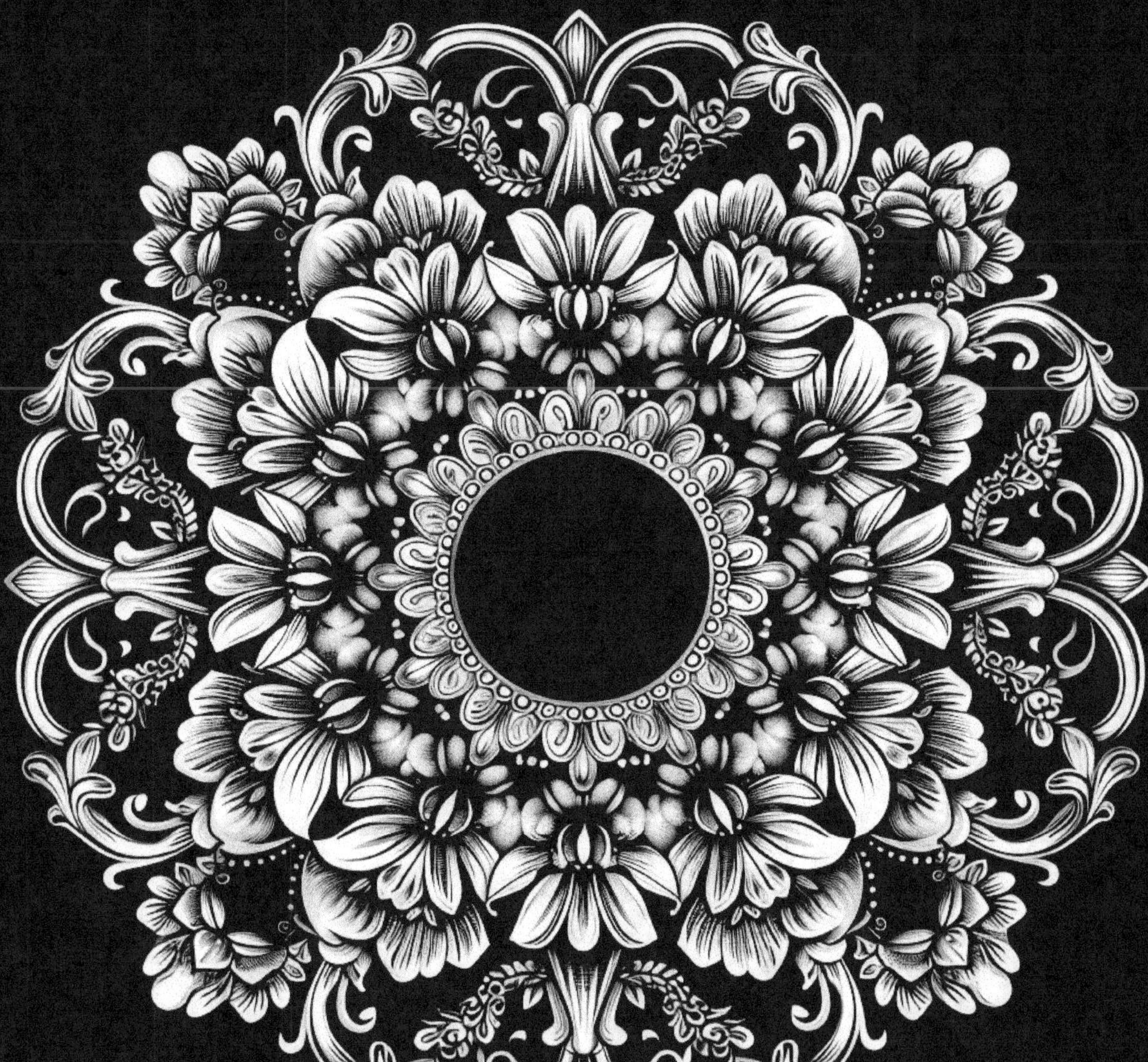

Beauty transforms the Soul

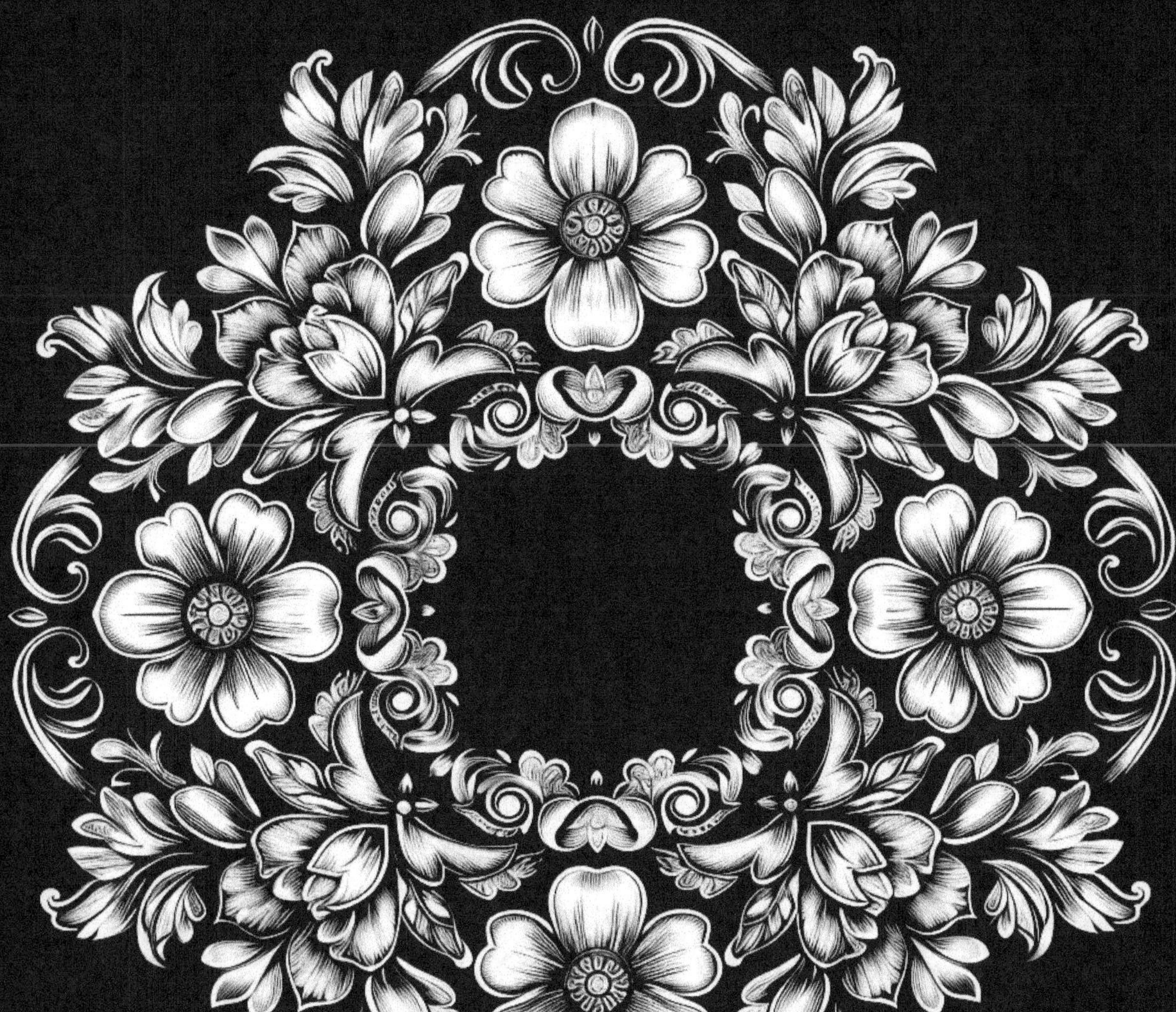

Beauty transforms the Soul

Beauty
transforms
the Soul

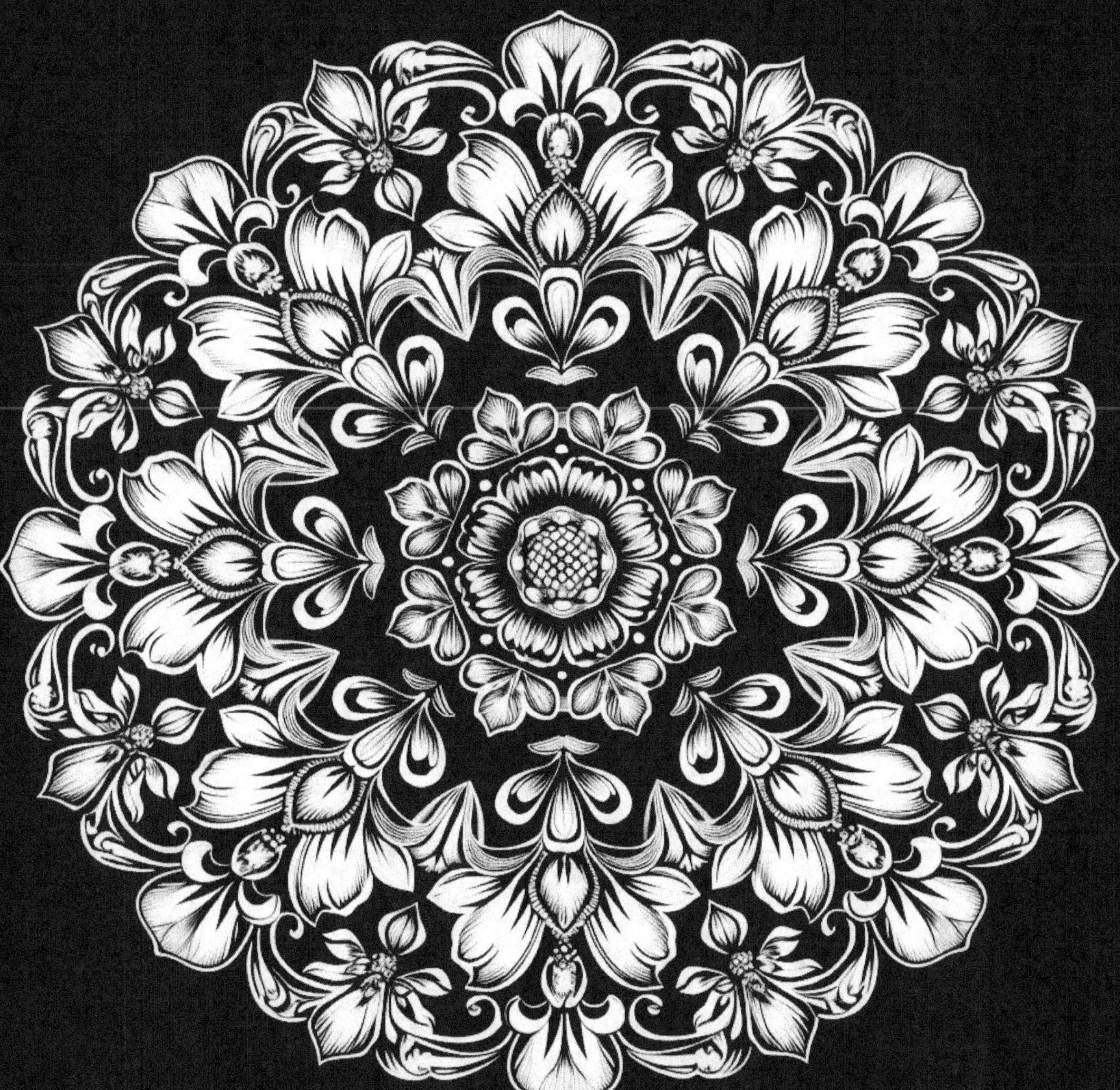

Beauty
transforms
the Soul

Beauty

transforms

the Soul

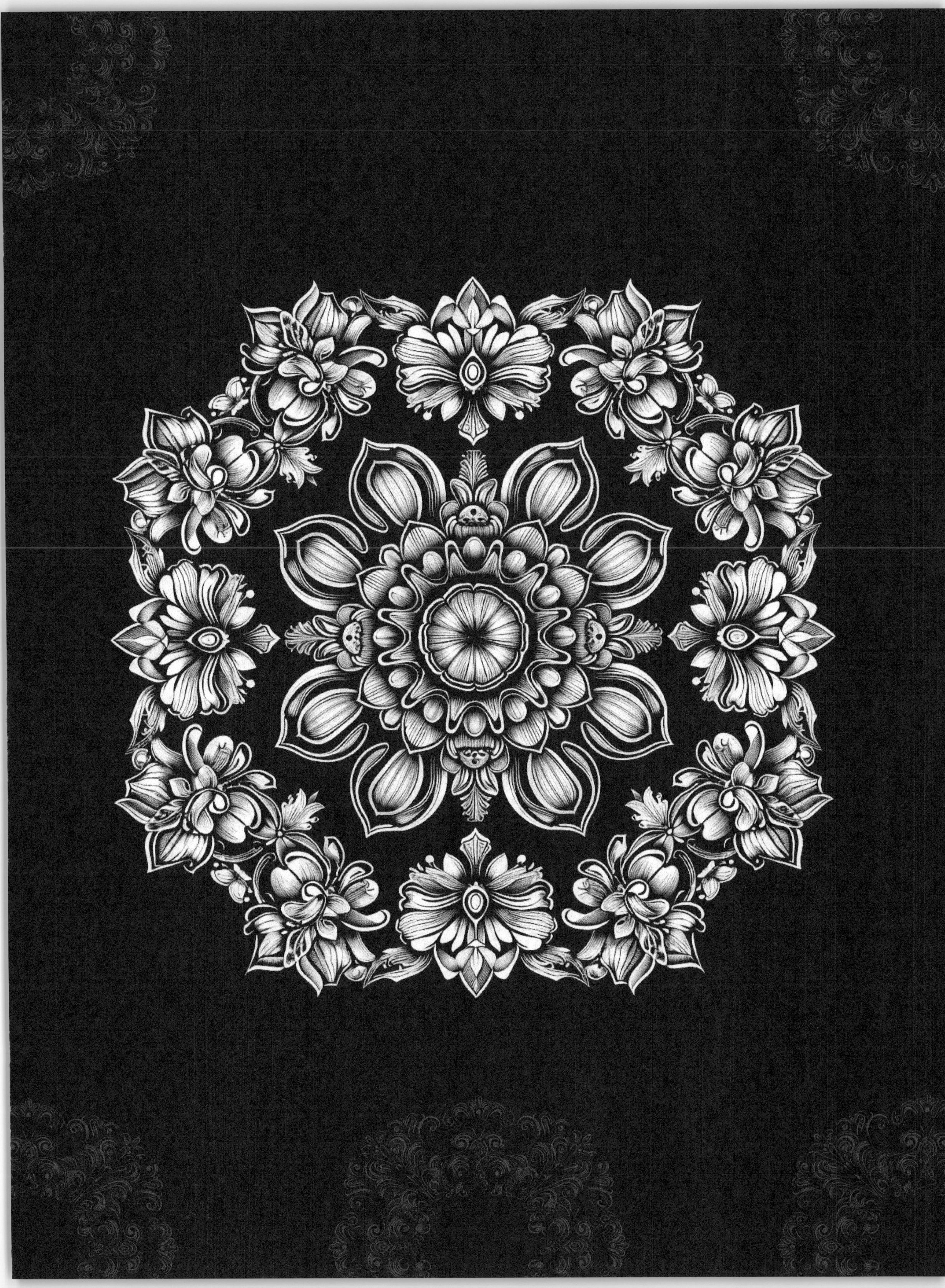

Beauty
transforms
the Soul

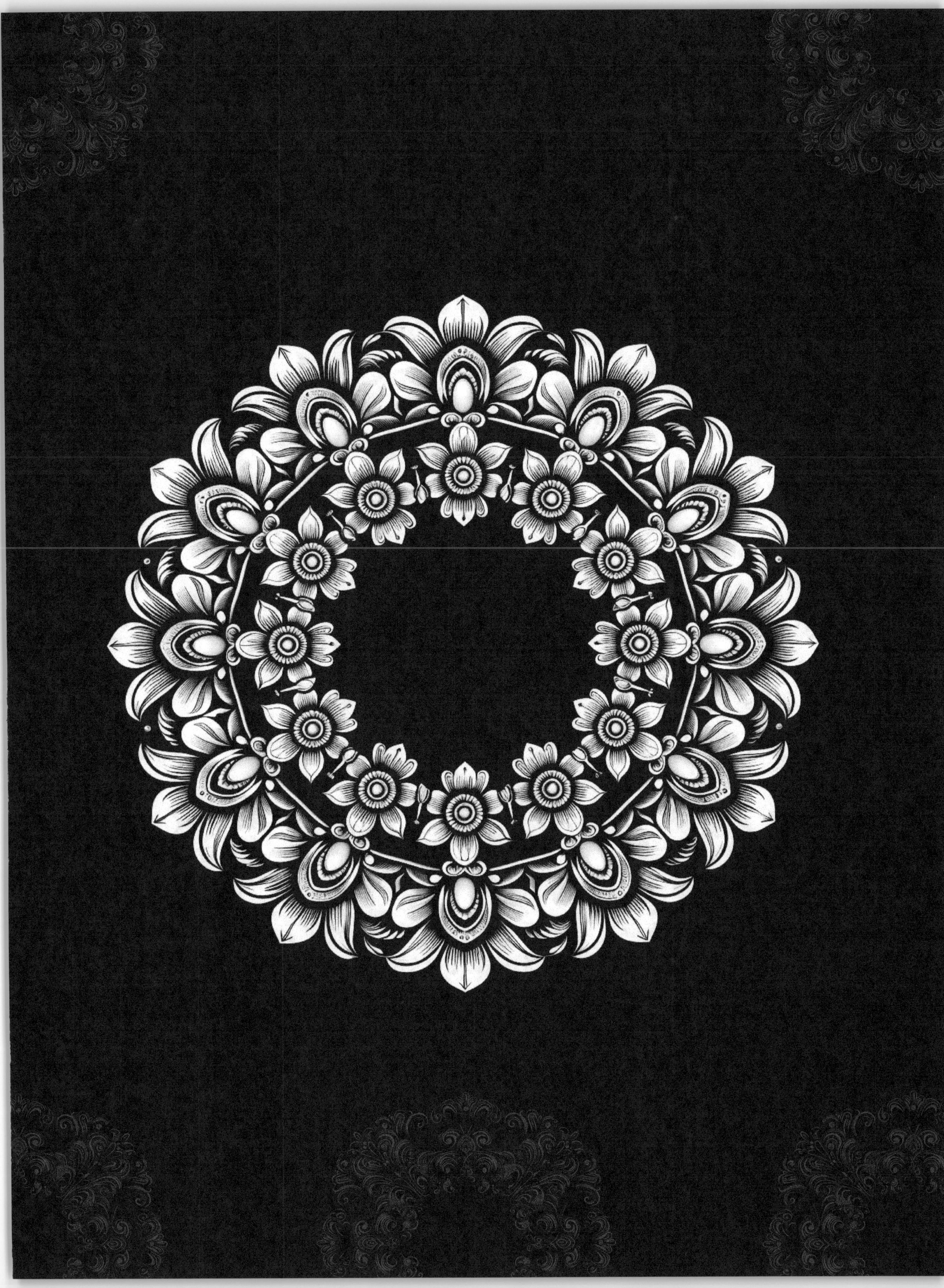

Beauty
transforms
the Soul

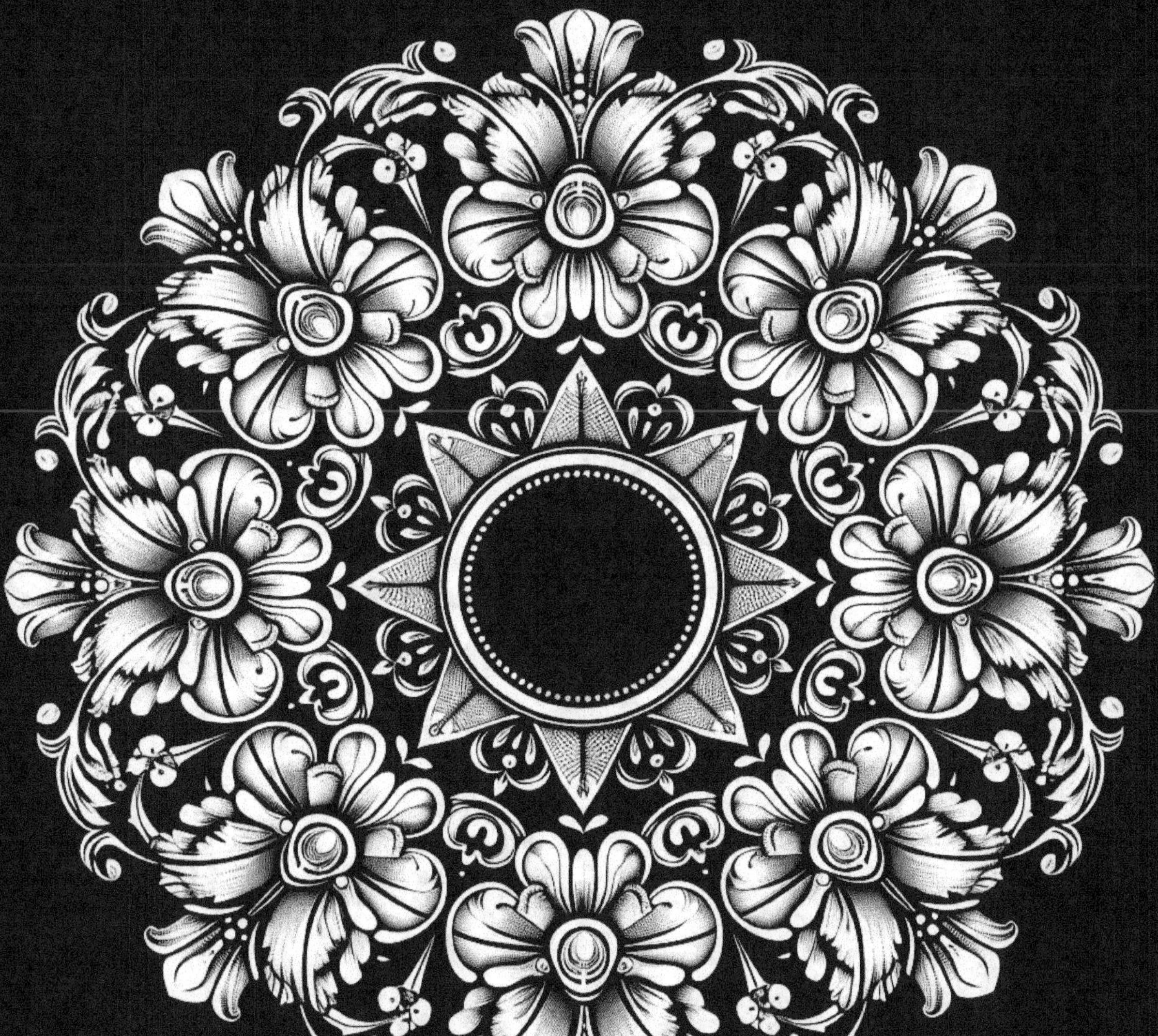

Beauty
transforms
the Soul

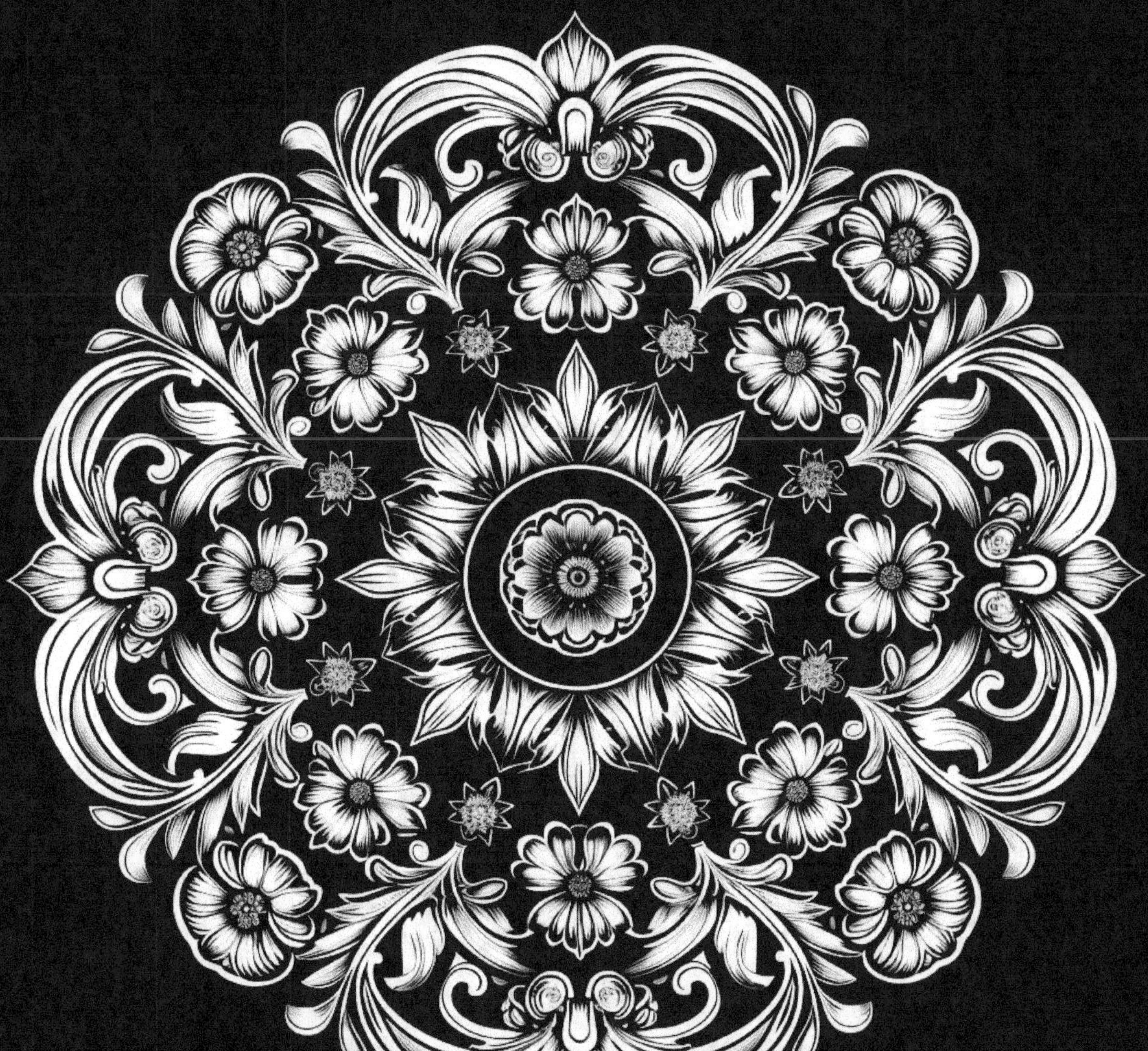

Beauty transforms the Soul

Beauty

transforms

the Soul

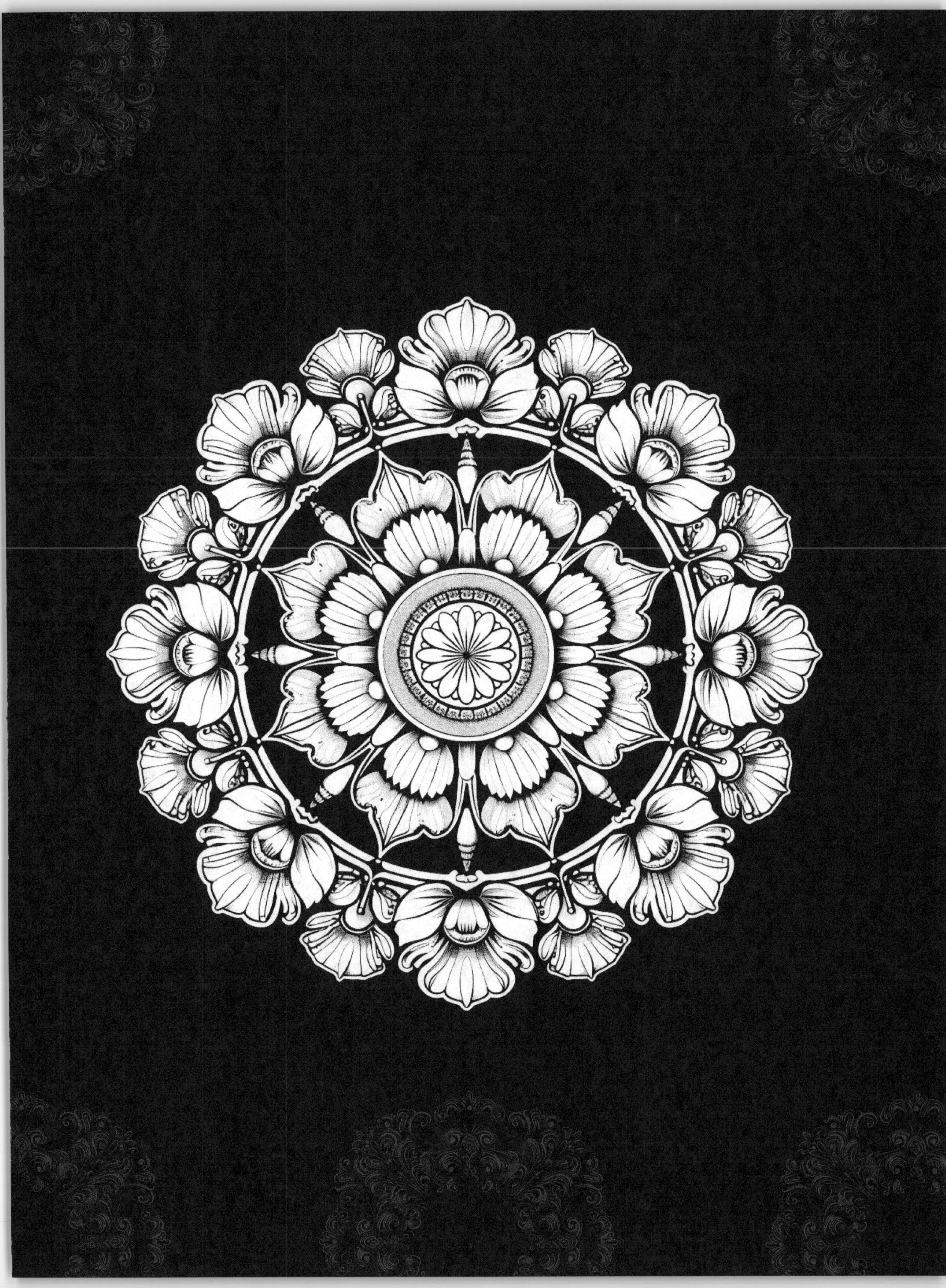

Beauty
transforms
the Soul

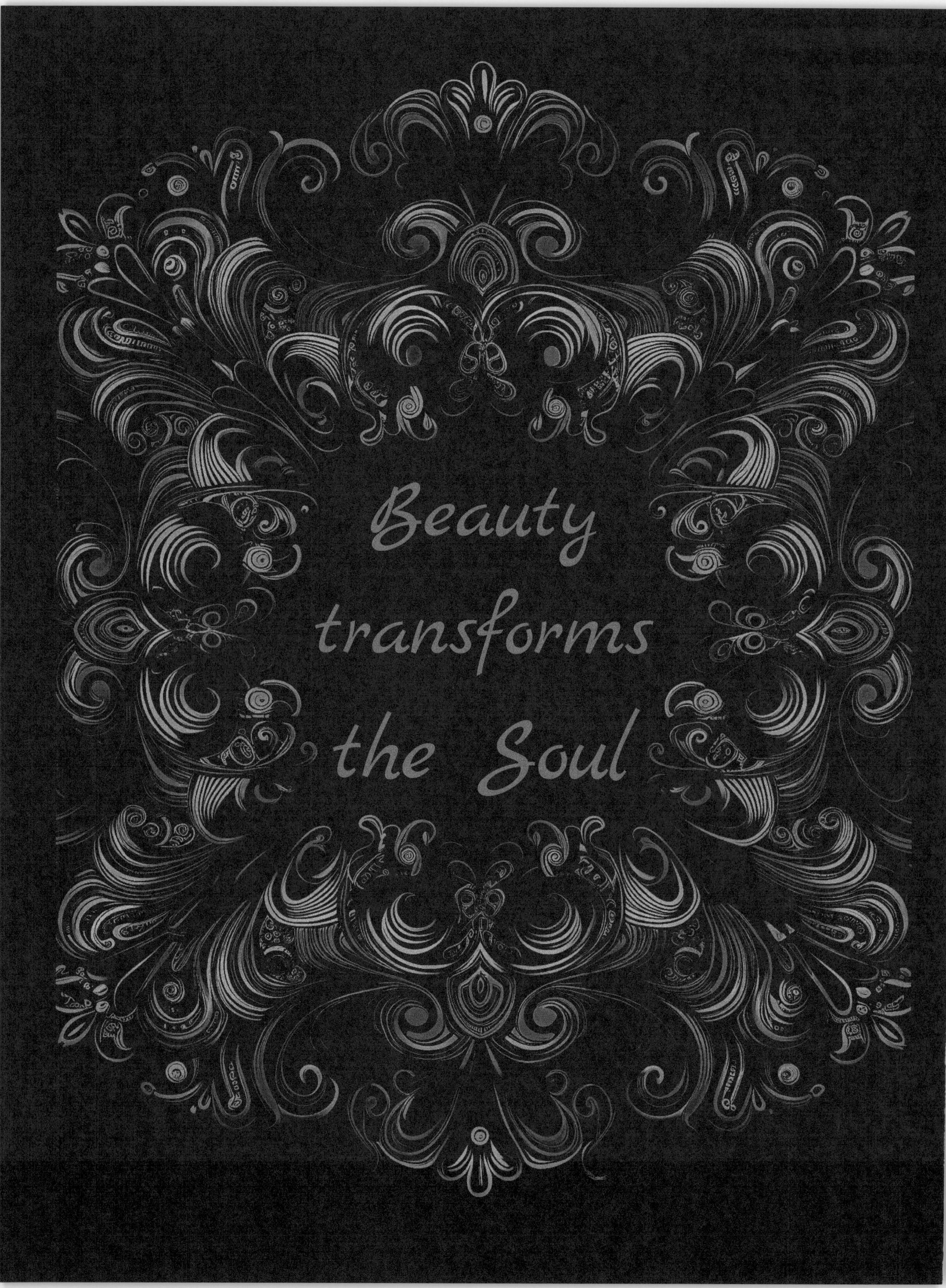
Beauty
transforms
the Soul

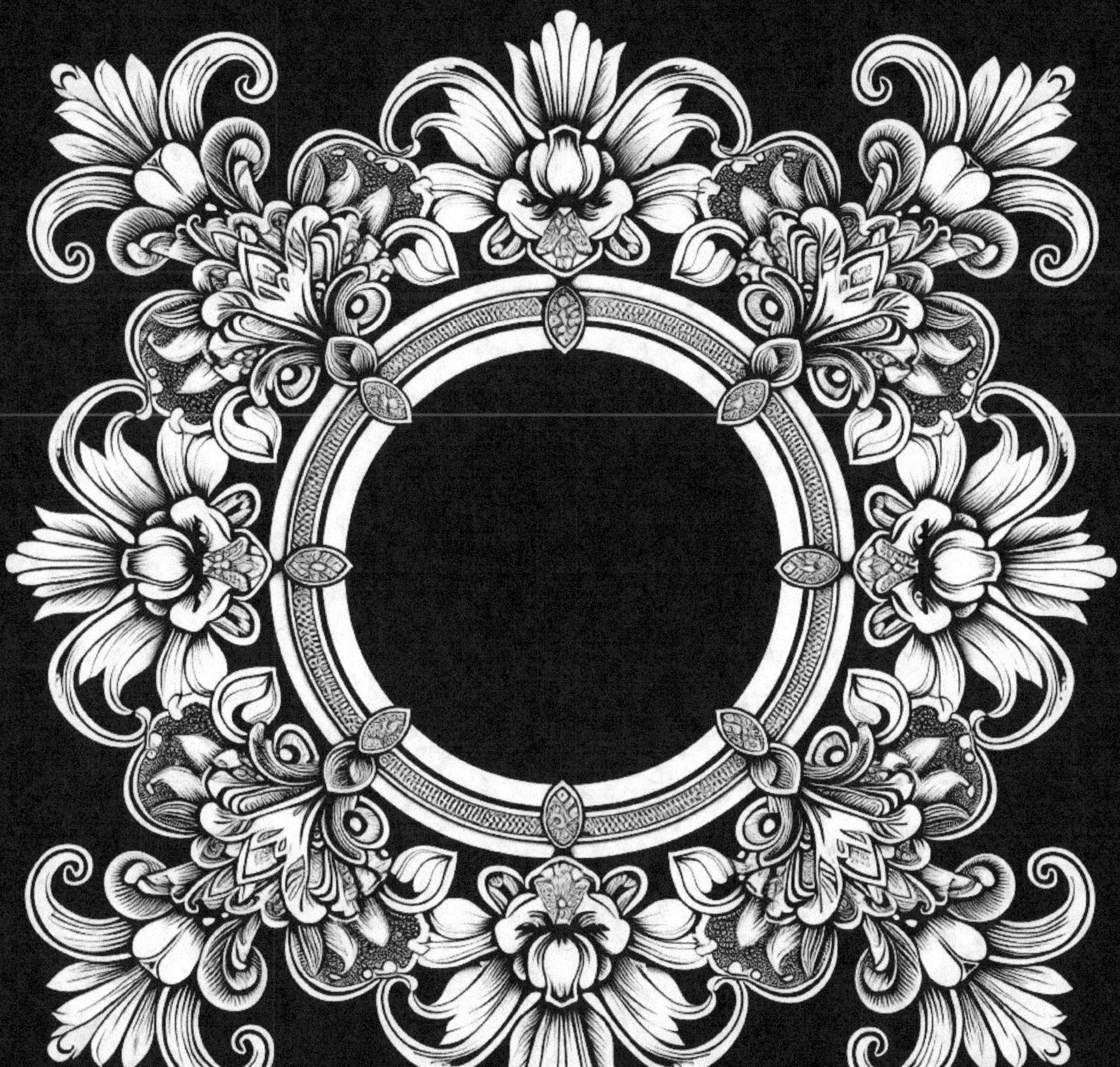

Beauty
transforms
the Soul

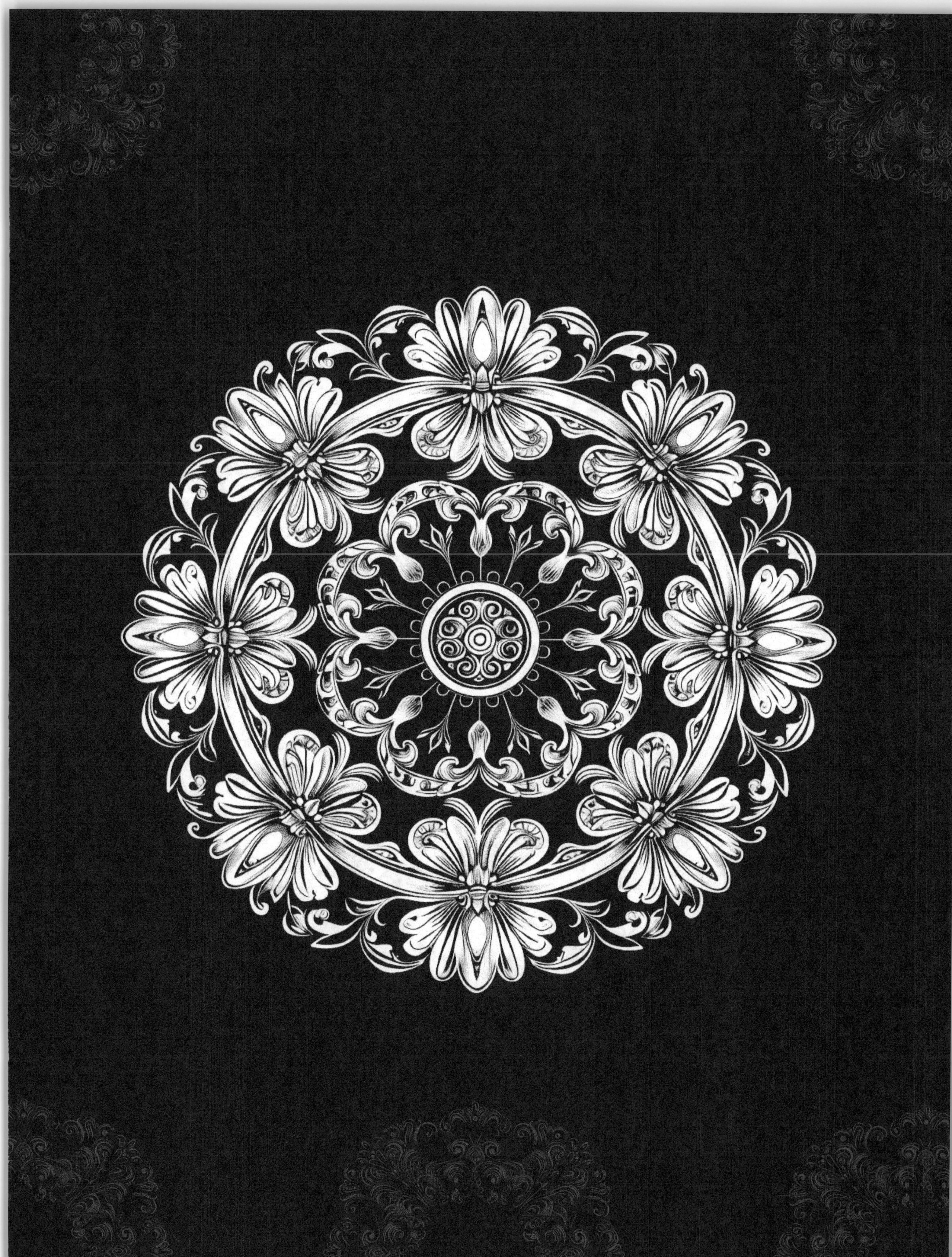

Beauty
transforms
the Soul

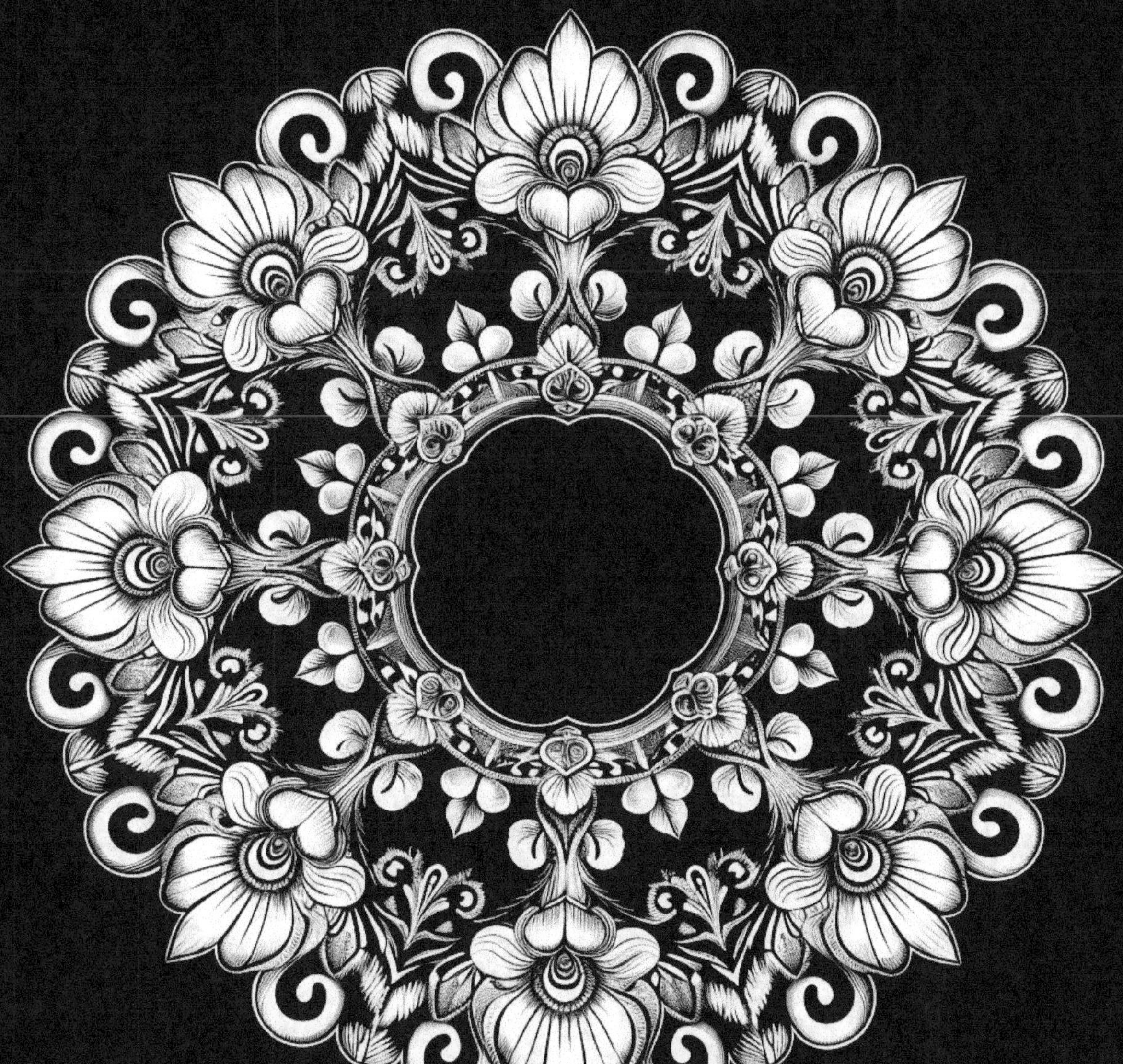

Beauty

transforms

the Soul

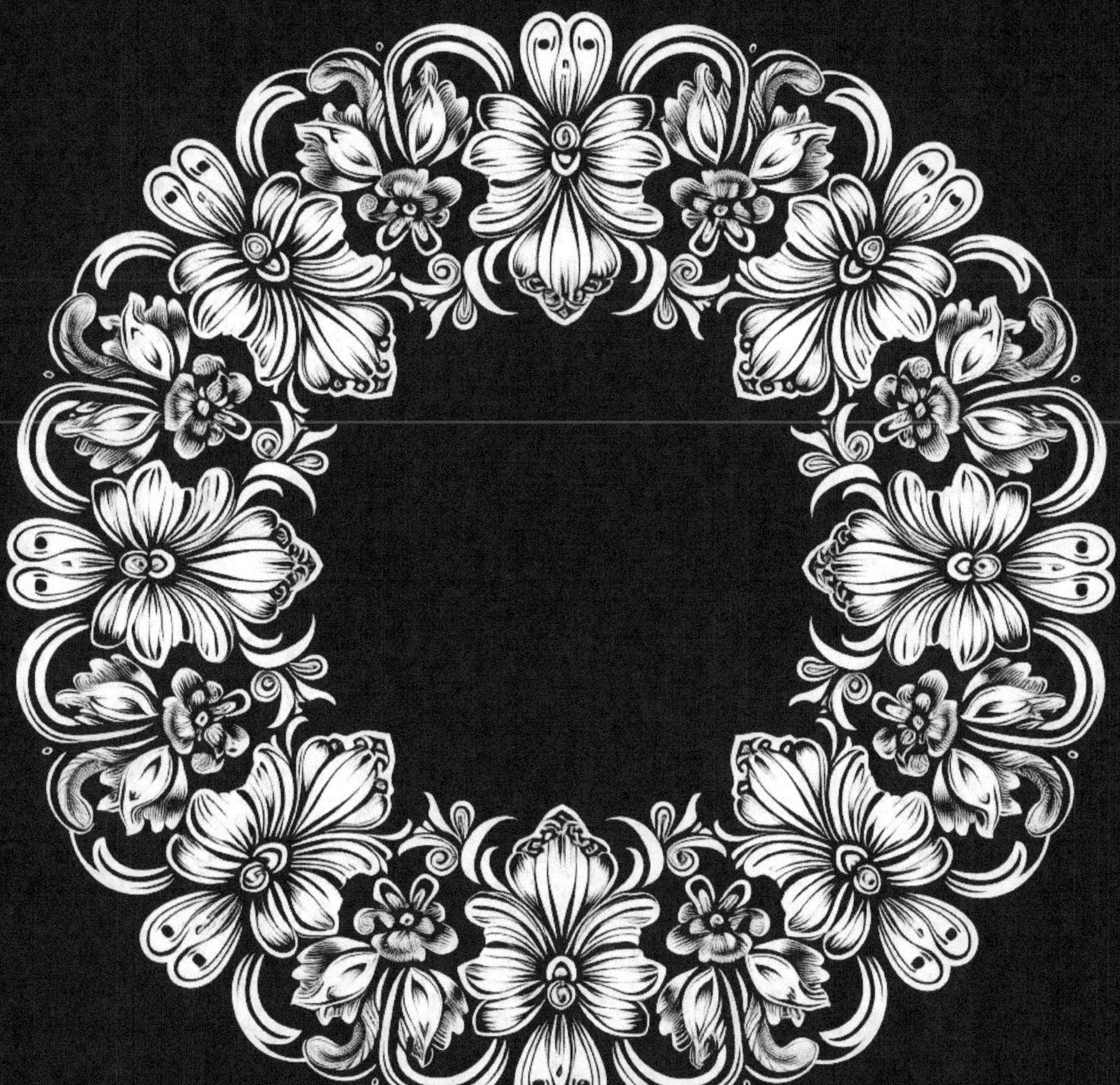

Beauty transforms the Soul

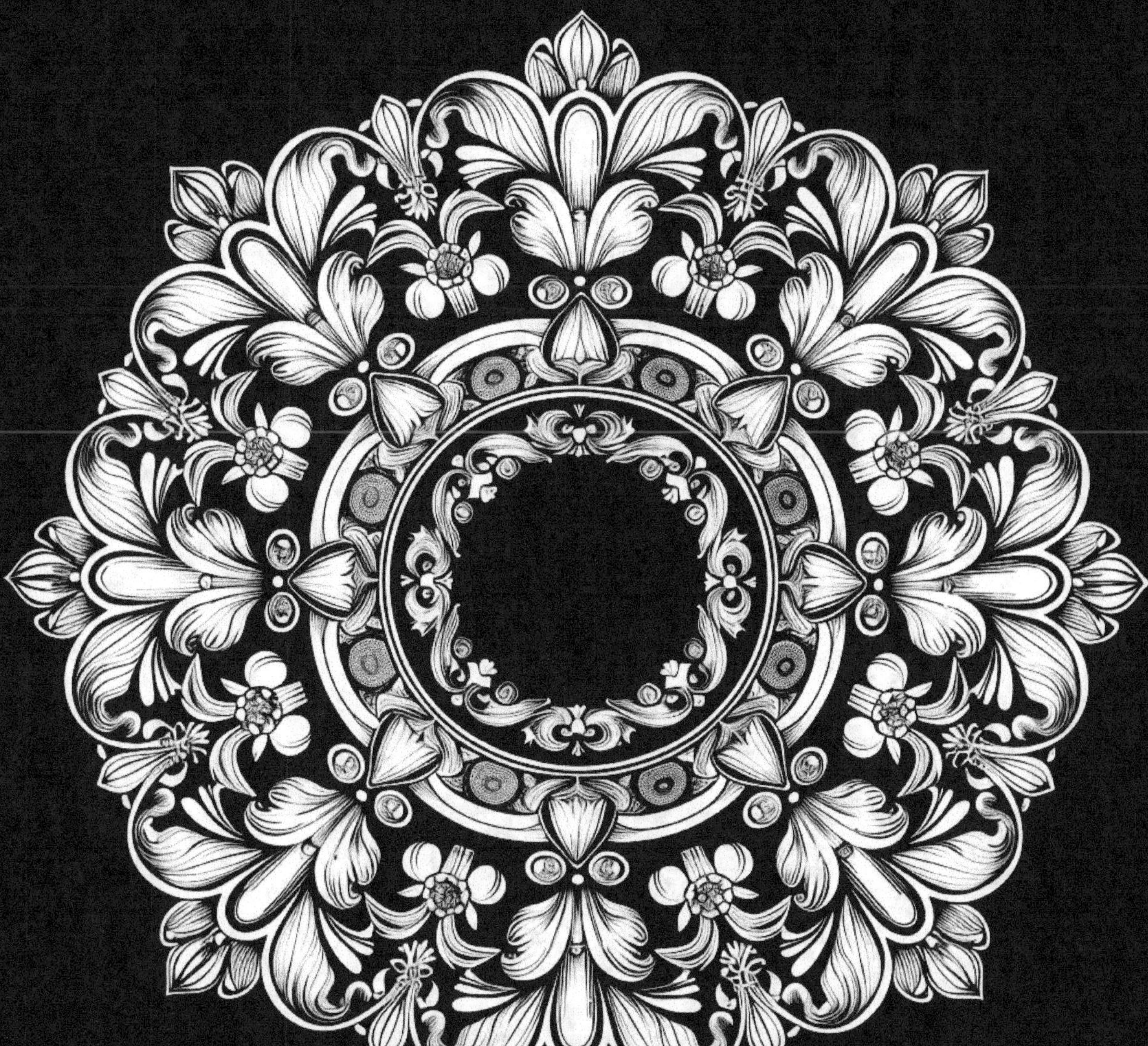

Beauty
transforms
the Soul

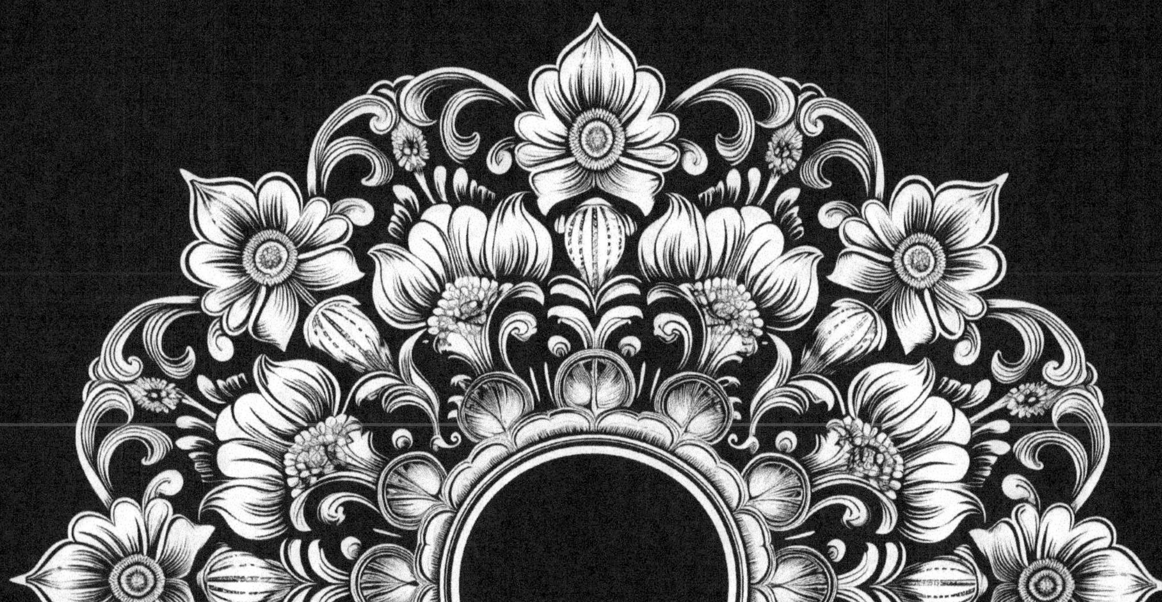

Beauty transforms the Soul

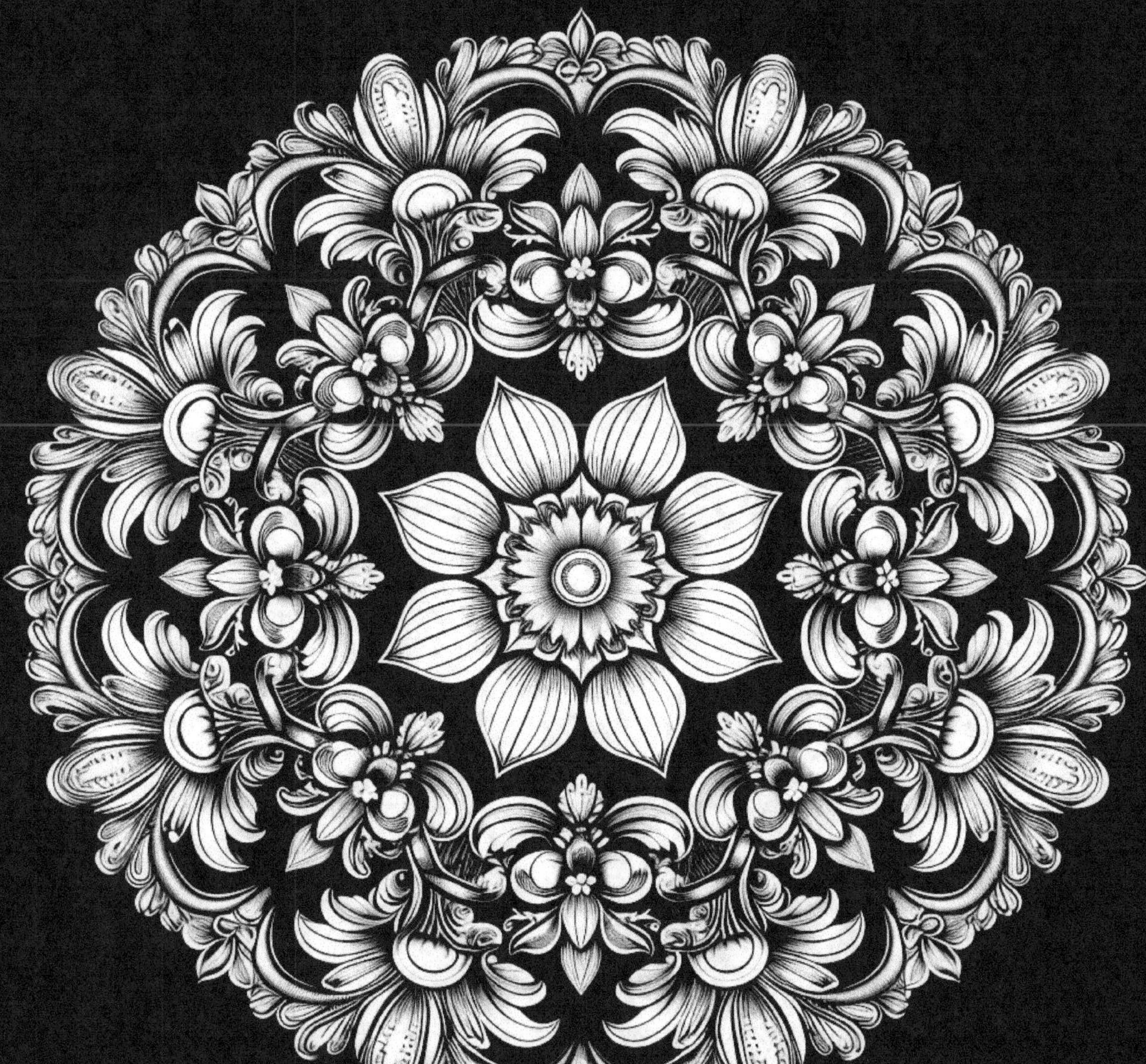

Beauty

transforms

the Soul

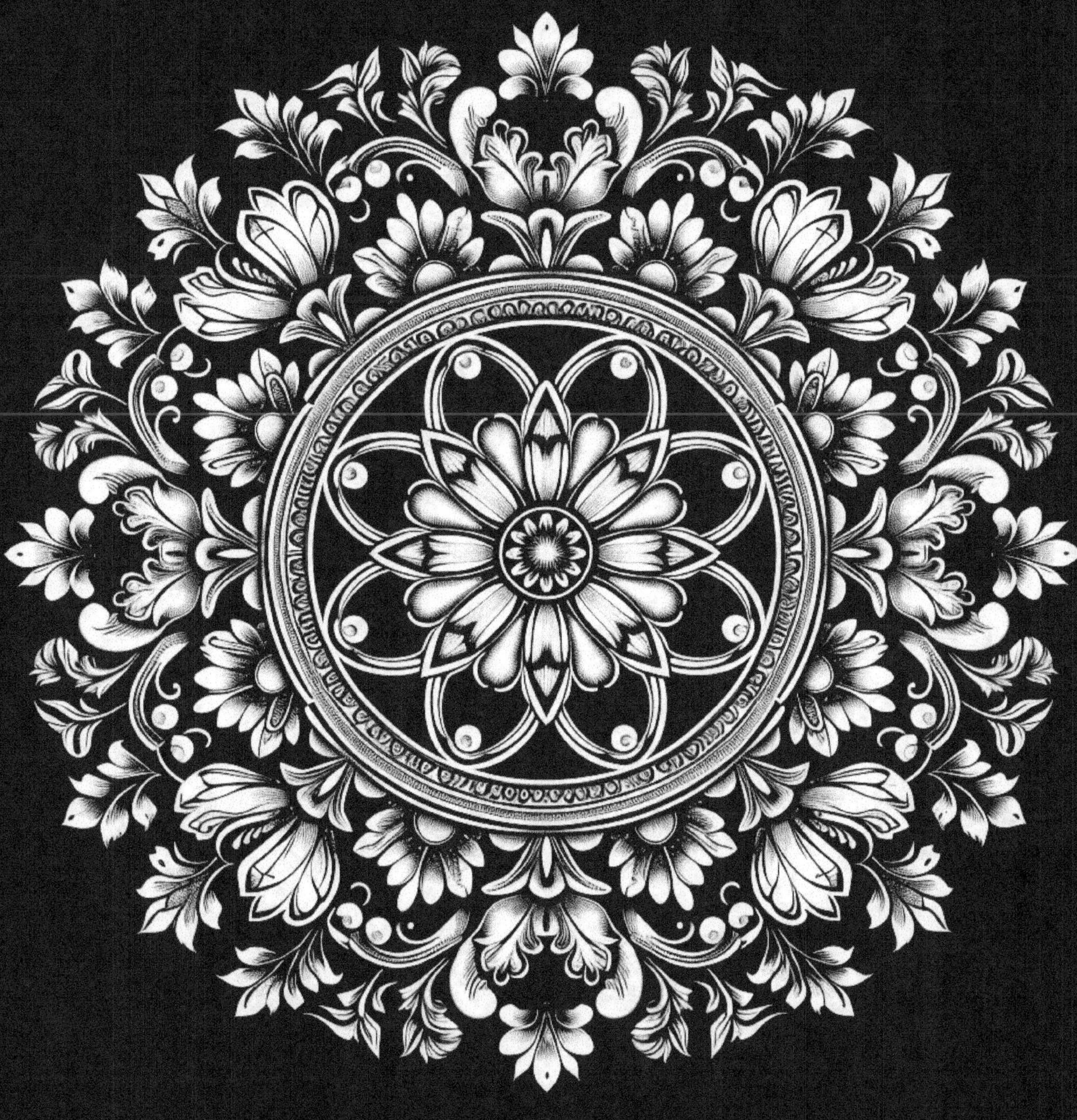

Beauty
transforms
the Soul

www.ingramcontent.com/pod-product-compliance
Lightning Source LLC
Chambersburg PA
CBHW081119240526
45470CB00019B/2628